**Proverbs 31 Men**
by John W. Stanko


ISBN 978-1-63360-158-1



For Worldwide Distribution
Printed in the U.S.A.

Urban Press
P.O. Box 8881
Pittsburgh, PA 15221-0881
412.646.2780
www.urbanpress.us

# Introduction

In 2018, I released a book titled *The Power of Purple: Women of Purpose in Scripture* and have wanted since then to produce a similar book for men. Around the time of the *Purple* release, I spoke at a church's men's event in another city, and I was struck by what I saw. The men were dull, almost asleep. They were nice enough, but they did not engage me or my topic. Now, that certainly could have been due to me or my topic, but that got me thinking about my encounters with men in general in various settings beyond that specific church:

- I have taught at a college where adults return to school to earn a degree. There were many classes in which women were about 90% of the students.
- I have done a few online classes on purpose and creativity during the 2020 pandemic, and again, it has been made up of 90% women.
- My church's choir before the pandemic was 80% women.

- I take annual trips to Kenya with a group interested in going with me and the last few years, the team going has been comprised of 90% women.

Now, this is hardly scientific research drawn from a large sample size and it could be unique to my experience—but I don't think so. In discussions with other pastors and life coaches, they have noticed the same trend. Therefore, I am concerned with how inactive and un-purposeful many church men are. I attribute this to one cause—fear—which of course a true man can usually never admit he has. He just soldiers on doing what he has always done, shrinking his world to its most manageable components so he does not encounter the failure or success of which he is terrified.

I want to challenge men to overcome their fears and lethargy to become more purposeful and I hope this book will help do that in some way. Of course, if men are not spiritually engaged in the things of the Lord, they are not going to read this book, but I write in faith and hope that God can get this book into the hands of men who need and are ready for it.

At first, I was considering calling the men's book *Men Like Mordecai* because we will get started by looking at Mordecai's purpose story. Then recently I was thinking and praying, and the thought came to me that we have made Proverbs 31 a chapter about women because it describes a wife of noble character. Yet the first nine verses of Proverbs 31 are addressed to someone named King Lemuel and the Proverbs 31 woman's husband was an elder at the gates of the city. Therefore, I have decided to extract some of the purpose material in Proverbs 31 where men are concerned and build on that from chapter to chapter.

I also don't want to write about the usual men of purpose like David, Moses, Paul, and others. I want to dig a bit deeper and look at Amos, Ezra, Matthew, Luke, Simon (not Peter), Philip the Evangelist, and Onesiphorus, just to name a few. As I did with my book *Success in Babylon*, I took each week's *Monday Memo* and made it a chapter in this book titled *Proverbs 31 Men: Brothers of Purpose in Scripture*. As was the case with the *Power of Purple*, the lessons we learn will apply to both men and women, but the focus will only be on male case studies.

To get ready for this theme, let me include the verses from Proverbs 31 that speak about and to men and then I will explain what I see in them indicating what God requires from men who are citizens of His kingdom:

> The sayings of King Lemuel—an inspired utterance his mother taught him. Listen, my son! Listen, son of my womb! Listen, my son, the answer to my prayers! Do not spend your strength on women, your vigor on those who ruin kings. It is not for kings, Lemuel—it is not for kings to drink wine, not for rulers to crave beer, lest they drink and forget what has been decreed, and deprive all the oppressed of their rights. Let beer be for those who are perishing, wine for those who are in anguish! Let them drink and forget their poverty and remember their misery no more. Speak up for those who cannot speak for themselves, for the rights of all who are destitute. Speak up and judge fairly; defend the rights of the poor and needy (Proverbs 31:1-9).
>
> Her husband is respected at the city gate, where he takes his seat among the elders of the land . . . Her children arise and call her blessed; her husband also, and he praises her: "Many women do noble things, but you surpass them all" (Proverbs 31:23, 28-29).

When I first considered this series, I thought I would be able to draw on the many *Monday Memos* I had already written about men of purpose, but I felt impressed not to do that. What I write in these pages will be all new material. I was excited to start but a bit apprehensive that I would be able to squeeze enough purpose insight from some of the lesser lights of biblical fame. The same God who has helped me write 975 *Memos* to date continued His support as I set my goal to search out and write a few more.

## God's Expectations

What do the verses above tell us about God's expectations for His male servants? It is said that there are three basic temptations for leaders who abuse their positions and they are sex, money, and power. Our fallen nature has found many ways to convert those temptations into sin. In Proverbs 31, we see at least two of those three temptations addressed: sex and power. Proverbs 31 contains the warnings of a mother to her son, urging him not to give his strength to women. If he doesn't learn to control his sexual urges, she warned him, he would cooperate with a weakness that has "ruined kings."

Most of the mother's warnings, however, focus on an abuse of power. Since men usually have the stronger muscle mass and larger physical stature, and since men have also historically held most of the leadership positions, this makes sense. Proverbs 31 warns men that their power is not to be used and abused and their judgment is not to be perverted by beer or wine, or any substance that could possibly blur their understanding of social justice and hinder their role in making justice a reality. These "kings" are to speak up for those who cannot speak for themselves. Men are to use their power to defend the rights of the poor and needy.

Now that women have more leadership positions available to them, the lessons are relevant for both men and women. God grants leaders power but expects them to use their power not to abuse or take advantage of others but to empower those who have no power. Later in Proverbs 31 when the noble wife is described, we read that her husband "takes his seat among the elders" and arises to call her [his wife] blessed." Male leaders are expected to place themselves where they can use their maturity and experience to help others, especially women and the poor.

## The Implications

My concern and the reason for this book is that I don't see enough men rising to God's expectations for service and leadership. As I began to write, I listened to the classic hymn, *Rise Up, Oh Men of God*, and reflected on the words:

> *Rise up, oh men of God, have done with lesser things. Give heart and soul and mind and strength to serve the King of Kings.*
>
> *Rise up, oh men of God, His Kingdom tarries long. Bring in the day of brotherhood, and end the night of wrong.*
>
> *Rise up, oh men of God, the Church for you doth wait. Send forth to serve the needs of men, in Christ our strength is great.*
>
> *Lift high the cross of Christ, tread where His feet have trod. As brothers of the Son of Man, rise up, oh men of God.*

There is a need for men to rise up as the song directs, but it seems many are called but few respond. In the first three chapters, we will look at Mordecai, Esther's protector and guardian, who in my estimation epitomizes the Proverbs 31 male. As we start, I ask that you examine your approach to power. Do you avoid or abuse it, or are you preparing to accept it and then deploy it for God's intended purposes? Along the way, we will examine other hindrances preventing men from rising up and I hope you are up to the task of finding and then fulfilling the purpose God has assigned you.

May this book help you to aspire to leadership and once there, to use the purpose power you have for the benefit of others. May God bless the reading and study of His Word!

John W. Stanko
Pittsburgh, PA
November 2020

# CHAPTER 1

## Sitting at the Gate

We need more men to step up and be involved in Kingdom work rather than simply working to make a living and trying to stay out of trouble. I don't believe I have ever heard or read a message based on the life of Mordecai. Even an online search yields little information about this man. I have heard him mentioned in the context of Esther's story, but there has been little focus on the one who adopted his cousin Esther (or Hadassah) after her parents died. Let's proceed and see what we can learn from Mordecai to help us in our purpose journeys, whether male or female.

### Sitting at the Gate

I mentioned in the Introduction what I noticed in Proverbs 31:23 about the husband of the Proverbs 31 woman: "Her husband is respected at the city gate, where he takes his seat among the elders of the land." We do not read that Mordecai was married, but we do learn that he sat in a place of responsibility as depicted in Proverbs 31:

> During the time Mordecai was sitting at the king's gate, Bigthana and Teresh, two of the king's officers

> who guarded the doorway, became angry and conspired to assassinate King Xerxes. But Mordecai found out about the plot and told Queen Esther, who in turn reported it to the king, giving credit to Mordecai. And when the report was investigated and found to be true, the two officials were impaled on poles. All this was recorded in the book of the annals in the presence of the king (Esther 2:21-23).

From that place and perspective, Mordecai played an important role in the protection not only of Esther but also of the king and ultimately all his fellow Jews. He was in the right place at the right time, paid attention to what he heard, and was a man of action—even though his action was that of a counselor and protector. This is more impressive when we see that Mordecai followed in the footsteps of Daniel:

> Now there was in the citadel of Susa a Jew of the tribe of Benjamin, named Mordecai son of Jair, the son of Shimei, the son of Kish, who had been carried into exile from Jerusalem by Nebuchadnezzar king of Babylon, among those taken captive with Jehoiachin king of Judah (Esther 2:5-6).

Mordecai was in a foreign land not by choice. He was exiled from his homeland to an idolatrous nation, but he determined to serve a useful purpose and not mourn the past or yearn for a better future. He started by caring for his cousin and his role grew from there. Your purpose makes you a leader, even if it is only the leadership of your local garden club. Why is that? It is because when you flow in purpose, you are in partnership with God, the One who assigned your purpose. He wants you to find and fulfill it more than you do, and when you accept who you are, He empowers you to fulfill it—whatever the "it" may be.

I have found too many men, and some women, who shun more responsibility. If they accept it, they may limit it to their own families but don't branch out to play a larger role in society. Some limit their leadership in their church, which is fine, but then if the church isn't growing, they stop growing or work to maintain the status quo instead of leading to cause change that will bring increase. Mordecai positioned *himself* (we do not see that the Lord placed him at the king's gate), paid attention to what he heard and saw, and God used him in a mighty way.

## Hiding or House Sitting?

Mordecai did not fade into obscurity after exile in his new venue. He did not form a Jews-only social club to maintain Jewish culture and worship. Mordecai took his turn to serve society at large at the king's gate, and God used and then blessed him. Eventually, Mordecai received wealth and honor not from a salary but as a blessing for the work he did that was not tied to a job description. He did not serve because he *had* to do so; he served because he *chose* to do so.

How about you? Are you serving beyond your own self interests? Is your goal to ensure that your tomorrow closely resembles today, or is it to launch out and play a change agent role that helps others through the power of your purpose and creativity? Are you sitting at the gate of responsibility or hiding in the shed of self-protection? I hope you will be a man, or a woman for that matter, like Mordecai, who is willing to serve at the highest level that your life preparation allows you to achieve.

# CHAPTER 2

## A Big Book and A Sharp Pencil

In the last chapter, we began looking at an often-overlooked hero in the Old Testament by the name of Mordecai. This man had no official title or power, yet time and again he positioned himself to be a blessing to those around him. He was not paid for the things he did; he just did them because they were the right things to do. He adopted his cousin, Esther, when her parents died and watched over her miraculous ascent to the throne. Then on more than one occasion, Mordecai was in the right place at the right time.

Mordecai was a political captive exiled to a foreign land the same way Daniel was. Both of them were carried away to Babylon against their will. All their dreams and aspirations were gone, never to be recovered. Mordecai could have been bitter or angry, but we see no evidence of that in the biblical narrative. Mordecai was not on anyone's payroll, so he was not being paid to be vigilant or kind. He was simply God's man who was directed by his values to do good, and God was watching and rewarded him in due time.

## The Plot

Like Daniel, Mordecai was a blessing not only to his own people but also to his captors, as we read in this story also included in Chapter One:

> During the time Mordecai was sitting at the king's gate, Bigthana and Teresh, two of the king's officers who guarded the doorway, became angry and conspired to assassinate King Xerxes. But Mordecai found out about the plot and told Queen Esther, who in turn reported it to the king, giving credit to Mordecai. And when the report was investigated and found to be true, the two officials were impaled on poles. All this was recorded in the book of the annals in the presence of the king (Esther 2:21-23).

Mordecai could have minded his own business, or he could have wished evil on his captors by staying silent concerning the plot he uncovered. Yet that would have been inconsistent with the characteristics of a Proverbs 31 man who we learned earlier, "Speak up for those who cannot speak for themselves, for the rights of all who are destitute. Speak up and judge fairly; defend the rights of the poor and needy" (Proverbs 31:8-9). Yes, it's true that the king in Susa was not defenseless or poor, but the plot to assassinate him was not ethical or just. Mordecai could not allow it to go unreported and so he acted, and the king was spared—and the assassins executed. End of story? Not quite, so let's read on.

## The Reward

We read this account in Esther 6:

> That night the king could not sleep; so he ordered the book of the chronicles, the record of his reign, to be brought in and read to him. It was found recorded there that Mordecai had exposed Bigthana and Teresh, two of the king's officers who guarded the doorway, who had conspired to assassinate King

> Xerxes. "What honor and recognition has Mordecai received for this?" the king asked. "Nothing has been done for him," his attendants answered (Esther 6:1-3).

The king could not sleep and thought of Mordecai. Can we assume God brought him to mind? When the king discovered nothing had been done to honor Mordecai for his loyalty, he set in motion a reward to rectify the oversight. We will see in the next chapter how this reward involved humiliating Mordecai's enemies, but for now, I want you to learn this lesson from the story so you can apply it to your own purpose journey. What the king did is a beautiful portrayal of our Lord, who is always watching and never forgets what His people do for His cause or in His name. The king rewarded Mordecai in due time, just like the Lord does His people:

> Do not be deceived: God cannot be mocked. A man reaps what he sows. Whoever sows to please their flesh, from the flesh will reap destruction; whoever sows to please the Spirit, from the Spirit will reap eternal life. Let us not become weary in doing good, for at the proper time we will reap a harvest if we do not give up. Therefore, as we have opportunity, let us do good to all people, especially to those who belong to the family of believers (Galatians 6:7-10).

When you flow in your purpose, you do what you do because you enjoy it and it is the right thing for you to do. You don't leave it up to someone else to do. It's not about career, promotion, or financial gain. It is to fulfill the truth found in Ephesians 2:10: "For we are God's handiwork, created in Christ Jesus to do good works, which God prepared in advance for us to do." This is important because modern culture stresses, even demands, that men pay attention to their work and give the best of who they are and what they have to their jobs. Then they have earned some down or leisure time and often they need it, because non-purposeful work takes more energy than it replenishes. That cultural scenario often prevents men from getting involved in good deeds like missions, service in the church, involvement in social justice, and care for the poor. They don't have time, energy, or courage to do what they do not get paid to do.

When men (or women) perform purpose work where they may not be a financial reward, God is watching. I have often said God has a big book and a sharp pencil and He writes it all down. Then one day, when we least expect it, He opens His book, like the king did with Mordecai, and settles all accounts. Mordecai cared for an orphan, served his people, and freely dispensed wisdom, and he did it all with grace and accuracy, and God, who cannot be out-given, repaid Him with interest.

May many more men like Mordecai rise up in these days to serve the cause of justice and help those in need, whether or not they have an official title and are paid to do so.

# CHAPTER 3

## Courage

I mentioned in chapter one that Mordecai's story was similar to Daniel's, for they were both in exile from their homeland, captives forced to leave their native land and live in Persia (modern Iran). This was not the only similarity, unfortunately, for just as Daniel was hated and resented in Babylon, the same was true for Mordecai. We read,

> After these events, King Xerxes honored Haman son of Hammedatha, the Agagite, elevating him and giving him a seat of honor higher than that of all the other nobles. All the royal officials at the king's gate knelt down and paid honor to Haman, for the king had commanded this concerning him. But Mordecai would not kneel down or pay him honor.
>
> Then the royal officials at the king's gate asked Mordecai, "Why do you disobey the king's command?" Day after day they spoke to him but he refused to comply. Therefore they told Haman about it to see whether Mordecai's behavior would be tolerated, for he had told them he was a Jew.

> When Haman saw that Mordecai would not kneel down or pay him honor, he was enraged. Yet having learned who Mordecai's people were, he scorned the idea of killing only Mordecai. Instead Haman looked for a way to destroy all Mordecai's people, the Jews, throughout the whole kingdom of Xerxes (Esther 3:1-6).

When Daniel faced his plot that led to the lion's den, he prayed. When Mordecai faced his crisis, he did the same thing:

> When Mordecai learned of all that had been done, he tore his clothes, put on sackcloth and ashes, and went out into the city, wailing loudly and bitterly. But he went only as far as the king's gate, because no one clothed in sackcloth was allowed to enter it. In every province to which the edict and order of the king came, there was great mourning among the Jews, with fasting, weeping and wailing. Many lay in sackcloth and ashes (Esther 4:1-3).

It was then that Mordecai uttered his oft-quoted advice to Esther in his appeal to her for help:

> When Esther's words were reported to Mordecai, he sent back this answer: "Do not think that because you are in the king's house you alone of all the Jews will escape. For if you remain silent at this time, relief and deliverance for the Jews will arise from another place, but you and your father's family will perish. And who knows but that you have come to your royal position for such a time as this?" (Esther 4:12-14).

## Courage and Action

Mordecai, like Daniel, showed great courage in a time of crisis. He knew his help came from the Lord, so he appealed directly to Him for help as his first order of business. This reminds me of what Moses said to Joshua: "Then Moses summoned Joshua and said to him in the presence of all Israel, '*Be strong and courageous*, for you must go with this people into the land that the Lord swore to their ancestors to give them, and you must divide it among them as their inheritance'" (Deuteronomy 31:7, emphasis added).

David gave his son Solomon this admonition in 1 Chronicles 28:20:

> David also said to Solomon his son, "*Be strong and courageous*, and do the work. Do not be afraid or discouraged, for the Lord God, my God, is with you. He will not fail you or forsake you until all the work for the service of the temple of the Lord is finished"

And Psalm 31:24 exhorts us to "*be strong and take heart*, all you who hope in the Lord."

I have learned in my lifetime that courage is not the absence of fear; it is learning to act in the midst of or despite fear. When people ask me if I am afraid to travel, I respond, "Yes, but I have learned to manage my fear (most of the time)." When I try a new project or write a book, the fear is there, but I work through it to act on my ideas. Sometimes when I am coaching someone else, I have to say the hard thing to them and I am afraid of how they will react. I have to press through the fear before it goes away, not waiting for it to subside.

We all need courage, but men are more prone to the effects of fear because we cannot admit we are afraid to maintain our facade of control and manliness. It was the women who were the first ones to Jesus' tomb while the men hid in fear in the Upper Room. Brothers, what is your purpose? Do you know? If you know, are you fulfilling it? If not, what are you afraid of? poverty? shame? ridicule?

Men of God, the Church needs you, the Lord needs you, and the sisters need you, not to be Superman, but to be yourself. God has more for you than staying out of trouble and attending church services. He has more for you than serving as an usher in your church for the next 10 years, telling the same people who sit in the same place every week what they can or cannot do (they already know). The world is waiting for you, but are you afraid to meet the world head on? It's time for you to take the missions trip, write the book, start the business, or do whatever else has resided in your heart and mind—probably for many years.

I implore you to face the reality and existence of your fear (I am sure Mordecai was afraid; otherwise, why would he have acted so swiftly to intercede for his people?) and take action, for faith without works or deeds is useless.

God needs His men to listen to David and Moses and take heart and courage to make a stand in their generation for Him, doing more than praying or giving a few dollars. We cannot allow the women to act alone. We must act as a team, seasoned by courage and motivated by love to be men and women of purpose to serve others.

# CHAPTER 4

## A Legacy of Service

We finished looking at Mordecai in the last chapter, and now I want to continue looking at good examples in the Bible of what I am calling Proverbs 31 men who model and epitomize the characteristics we learned men should have as described in Proverbs 31. Those traits include:

1. Using leadership power to benefit and not harm those who are weaker.
2. Being concerned for social justice.
3. Honoring women.
4. Serving in leadership capacities as "elders at the gate," where wisdom and justice are dispensed.

In this chapter, let's look at a man whose name is mentioned only twice by Paul, those being in his second letter to Timothy. That man's name was Onesiphorus.

### Who Was That Man?

We read in 2 Timothy 1:15-18:

You know that everyone in the province of Asia has

> deserted me, including Phygelus and Hermogenes. May the Lord show mercy to the household of **Onesiphorus**, because he often refreshed me and was not ashamed of my chains. On the contrary, when he was in Rome, he searched hard for me until he found me. May the Lord grant that he will find mercy from the Lord on that day! You know very well in how many ways he helped me in Ephesus (emphasis added).

While it seems that all others were abandoning or ignoring Paul, this man Onesiphorus did practical things to refresh Paul. When Paul was imprisoned in Rome, Onesiphorus risked disfavor with the authorities by admitting that he was a friend of their state prisoner and went out of his way to find Paul and minister to his needs. It seems it was not such an easy task to find Paul, but Onesiphorus persevered and located the man of God who needed some encouragement and companionship. Paul summarized what Onesiphorus did in one word (mercy) and prayed that God would fulfill a promise Jesus made for him and his household: "Blessed are the merciful, for they will be shown mercy" (Matthew 5:7).

## What Can We Learn?

We learn from Onesiphorus' example that Proverbs 31 men are concerned about and nurture relationships. He was not only task oriented but also exerted great energy to sustain and maintain the friendship he had with Paul, even though Paul could in no way return the blessing. First Onesiphorus had to exert much effort in finding Paul in Rome and then serving him as Paul needed, not as was convenient for Onesiphorus. Because he had a heart to serve, Onesiphorus found "many ways" to help Paul while they were in Ephesus.

Proverbs 31 men must follow in Onesiphorus' footsteps and use their strength not to cheer on their favorite sports team or build a world of comfort and convenience for themselves. All of us, men and women, must find practical ways to serve others, which may not always be convenient or in our own neighborhood or country. We cannot over-spiritualize the process of blessing others but should work to meet their needs in the love of Christ, regardless of how difficult it may be or how much time and energy we must expend to find and then meet the needs of others.

As Paul closed his letter, he directed Timothy to "greet Priscilla and Aquila and the household of Onesiphorus" (2 Timothy 4:19). Onesiphorus had stored up a inheritance of blessing for his family, which indicates we are not certain if he was still alive when Paul wrote the letter. Whether he was or not, the point is that Onesiphorus was a blessing to his household because he was a blessing to others. We have to assume he displayed the same mercy to those closest to him as he did to Paul.

Are you laying up a deposit your family can draw on that comes from doing good deeds? Are you willing to devote energy and time to the care of others? Are you interested in power so you can have a title and "be somebody," or are you willing to use your power to encourage and empower others?

Onesiphorus is mentioned in God's inspired Word not because he preached great messages or taught deep truths. He is mentioned because he helped a friend in his friend's hour of desperate need while God was watching. May you devote your life toward the same objective, and may God watch and bless you and yours as you distinguish yourself through a life of selfless service—like Proverbs 31 men are expected to do

# CHAPTER 5

## Social Justice

Let's continue our study with a look at one of the minor prophets named Amos. (Keep in mind that these prophets considered "minor" received that label due to the shortness of their biblical accounts and in no way denigrates their message or impact.) Keep in mind that we are looking at men who modeled certain behaviors described in Proverbs 31, which include:

1. Using leadership power to benefit and not harm those who are weaker.
2. Being concerned for social justice.
3. Honoring women.
4. Serving in leadership capacities as "elders at the gate," where wisdom and justice are dispensed.

My goal is to stir up readers who are willing to emulate the behavior and lifestyle of these Proverbs 31 men we study. Let's get started.

### Who Was This Man?

Amos was a shepherd: "The words of Amos, one of

the shepherds of Tekoa" (Amos 1:1). He was also a farme "I was neither a prophet nor the son of a prophet, but I was shepherd, and I also took care of sycamore-fig trees" (Am 7:1). He was not numbered among the officially recognize prophets in either the southern kingdom where two trib lived (Judah) or the northern kingdom (Israel) where the othe ten tribes resided. Yet Amos responded to the call and word c the Lord to leave the southern kingdom to go deliver a mes sage to the northern kingdom, where he quickly wore out hi welcome.

It seems that the northern kingdom was experiencin unprecedented economic prosperity but had forgotten socia justice and the rights of the poor in their drive to amass wealth Amos began by prophesying against Israel's neighbors but then took dead aim at God's people and told them disaster was coming because of their wicked ways:

> "There are those who hate the one who upholds justice in court and detest the one who tells the truth. You levy a straw tax on the poor and impose a tax on their grain. Therefore, though you have built stone mansions, you will not live in them; though you have planted lush vineyards, you will not drink their wine. For I know how many are your offenses and how great your sins. There are those who oppress the innocent and take bribes and deprive the poor of justice in the courts. Therefore the prudent keep quiet in such times, for the times are evil" (Amos 5:10-13).

## Some Thoughts

Here are some thoughts on Amos and his mission that can help all people, especially men, in their attempt to carry out their God-given purpose in these days.

1. Amos was not only "interested" in his people of the southern tribe but had a worldview that

allowed him to address the nations around Israel as well as his northern cousins. We also need to be world Christians and not only interested in our nation or culture.

2. Amos had visions and wrote poetry. Like King David, he obviously nurtured his creativity so that when God spoke to him, he was prepared to speak and write because he had practiced and worked at it to sharpen his skills. We also need to hone our creativity by working at it.

3. Like Jesus, Amos drew on analogies and images from his work world of shepherding and farming. For example,

   > This is what the Sovereign Lord showed me: a basket of ripe fruit. "What do you see, Amos?" he asked. "A basket of ripe fruit," I answered. Then the Lord said to me, "The time is ripe for my people Israel; I will spare them no longer" (Amos 8:1-2).

   This indicates he paid attention to and meditated on what he heard and saw in the Lord and then put some thought, inspired by the Spirit, to communicate important lessons for the people to hear. We need to use social media and other means to share what the Lord is showing us.

4. Amos was a "kingdom" man and not a "church" man. His loyalty was to Yahweh, the King of Israel, and not to his "denomination" or his tribal people. That is why he was ostracized but stayed true to his calling when he was evicted. It is not enough to attend church; we must represent Christ beyond church to the world at large by whatever means the Lord provides.

5. Amos urged Israel to build relationships with

the poor, thus breaking down the barriers between the rich and poor, who were (and are) equal in the sight of God. We need to invest our discretionary money not on sports, tattoos, gambling, or entertainment, but rather on the oppressed and needy.

## Implications for Us

The problem is that when we talk of justice, people often politicize the discussion. Since everyone has an opinion about what is just and right, there is seldom agreement about the best behavior or course of action. Consider the issue of health care as an example. Some believe the government should pay for most if not all of health care and others believe it should be based more on a free market approach that does indeed create inequities. Both sides blast away at the other side, one claiming the other is socialist and the other claiming those who disagree are racist or at least insensitive (I know this is a gross oversimplification.)

The point is that each man must seek the Lord to help him define the issues of justice and mercy. Then once he has his definition, he must not rail against those who disagree with him but rather *do* something with what he sees. For instance, I decided to become a university instructor among the poor who decided to return to school and I served in that capacity for 22 years. I also founded a publishing company that provides services to those who have a story but cannot always pay for those services. I attend a church that is active in the community around the church building to help the poor. Finally, my work in Africa among the poor there is well chronicled.

What are you doing to help the poor and contribute to social justice, not just among your own people or with your own political affiliations, but through your church? If your church isn't doing much, what is your response? Do you do nothing as well, or can you be like Amos who, although a blue-collar worker, decided to do something by relocating and speaking out against the abuses of his day (this was not politically motivated and was not directed at his enemies)?

If we are going to be Proverbs 31 men, then we must be involved at a grass-roots level, not simply as rabble-rousers (talk is cheap and ideas cheaper) but as involved individuals who model what we teach and practice what we preach.

# CHAPTER 6

## A Man of the Word

Let's continue our study of Proverbs 31 men in this chapter with a look at an obscure Old Testament priest named Ezra. By way of reminder, the purpose of this book is to look at men who modeled certain behaviors described in Proverbs 31, which include:

1. Using leadership power to benefit and not harm those who are weaker.
2. Being concerned for social justice.
3. Honoring women.
4. Serving in leadership capacities as "elders at the gate," where wisdom and justice are dispensed.

Ezra does not qualify on all the points above, but he excelled in leading his people because of his superb knowledge of the Word, which will be the focus of this discussion.

### Who Was This Man?

Ezra was a priest who was in Babylon, taken there under the same conditions as Daniel:

> After these things, during the reign of Artaxerxes king of Persia, Ezra son of Seraiah, the son of Azariah, the son of Hilkiah, the son of Shallum, the son of Zadok, the son of Ahitub, the son of Amariah, the son of Azariah, the son of Meraioth, the son of Zerahiah, the son of Uzzi, the son of Bukki, the son of Abishua, the son of Phinehas, the son of Eleazar, the son of Aaron the chief priest—this Ezra came up from Babylon (Ezra 7:1-6a).

Ezra was selected to lead the contingent returning to Jerusalem having distinguished himself as a man of the Word:

- He was a teacher well versed in the Law of Moses, which the Lord, the God of Israel, had given (Ezra 7:6b).
- This is a copy of the letter King Artaxerxes had given to Ezra the priest, a teacher of the Law, a man learned in matters concerning the commands and decrees of the Lord for Israel: Artaxerxes, king of kings, To Ezra the priest, teacher of the Law of the God of heaven (Ezra 7:11-12).
- Now I, King Artaxerxes, decree that all the treasurers of Trans-Euphrates are to provide with diligence whatever Ezra the priest, the teacher of the Law of the God of heaven, may ask of you (Ezra 7:21).

The Persian king had heard of Ezra because he had distinguished himself as a Bible scholar who taught others the Word:

> And you, Ezra, in accordance with the wisdom of your God, which you possess, appoint magistrates and judges to administer justice to all the people of Trans-Euphrates—all who know the laws of your God. And you are to teach any who do not know

> them. Whoever does not obey the law of your God and the law of the king must surely be punished by death, banishment, confiscation of property, or imprisonment (Ezra 7:25-26).

Ezra had so completely given himself to the study of God's word that he was known not only among the Jews but also among the heathen as a learned man. On that basis, he was chosen to serve his people by leading them back to rebuild Jerusalem, the city of their fathers.

### Men of the Word

I recently met with someone who told me they studied the Word of God two to three hours almost every day. When I asked him the reason why, he said, "So I can know the Word." While I was impressed with this person's diligence and commitment, I challenged him to be more than a man of the Word. I urged him to become a teacher of the Word, for that is what a Proverbs 31 man needs to be. If we are to dispense justice and lead people, we must not only know the Word but also obey the Word, teach the Word, and also apply the principles found in the Word to real-life situations.

I am concerned because so few men are involved in their churches teaching others, especially children. I am concerned that men seem more entranced by sports and other "manly" activities than they are immersed in the Word—but not just immersed to build themselves up but to teach others as well. I am also concerned that I see men more energized by politics on social media who are sharing their political insights rather than their insights into God's word (including pastors).

Ezra had a wonderful reputation as a man of wisdom as the king stated in his memo: "And you, Ezra, in accordance with the wisdom of your God, which you possess . . ." (Ezra 7:25a). Where are the men of wisdom today? Where are the men who are available to be drafted to lead God's people because they know the Word, not because they are successful businessmen or sports trivia champions?

I go back to the song I quoted in the first chapter titled *Rise Up, Oh Men of God.* The stanzas go like this:

> *Rise up, Oh men of God, have done with lesser things. Give heart and soul and mind and strength, to serve the King of Kings.*
>
> *Rise up, Oh men of God, His Kingdom tarries on. Bring in the day of brotherhood, and end the night of wrong.*
>
> *Rise up, oh men of God, the Church for you doth wait. Send forth to serve the needs of men, in Christ our strength is great.*
>
> *Lift high the Cross of Christ, tread where His feet have trod. As brothers of the Son of Man, rise up oh men of God.*

How many men will commit to be people of the Word not only to obey it but also to teach it? If you are ready to make that commitment, then the time to start is now, for every day counts as we rise up to serve this generation as God would have us do. Every day counts if you are going to follow in Ezra's footsteps to be a man of the Word.

# CHAPTER 7

## In the Spirit

So far, in our Proverbs 31 Men series, we have looked at Mordecai, Onesiphorus, Amos, and Ezra, examining what made these individuals stand out as men of purpose. Let's move on and look at a man named Simeon, of which we know very little—but what we do know tells us a lot:

> Now there was a man in Jerusalem called Simeon, who was righteous and devout. He was waiting for the consolation of Israel, and the Holy Spirit was on him. It had been revealed to him by the Holy Spirit that he would not die before he had seen the Lord's Messiah. Moved by the Spirit, he went into the temple courts. When the parents brought in the child Jesus to do for him what the custom of the Law required, Simeon took him in his arms and praised God, saying: "Sovereign Lord, as you have promised, you may now dismiss your servant in peace. For my eyes have seen your salvation, which you have prepared in the sight of all nations: a light for revelation to the Gentiles, and the glory of your people Israel."

> The child's father and mother marveled at what was said about him. Then Simeon blessed them and said to Mary, his mother: "This child is destined to cause the falling and rising of many in Israel, and to be a sign that will be spoken against, so that the thoughts of many hearts will be revealed. And a sword will pierce your own soul too" (Luke 2:25-35).

There is a phrase that stands out in those verses, so let's begin our study there as we examine what it was like for Simeon to be a man of the Holy Spirit.

## In the Spirit

Notice that we learn three things about Simeon and his relationship with the Holy Spirit:

1. The Holy Spirit was on him.
2. The Holy Spirit had revealed something to him.
3. The Holy Spirit moved him to go to the Temple to meet the baby Jesus.

Obviously, the Holy Spirit was active and working in Simeon's life, but we are not told how or why. We do not know if there were any other Spirit manifestations or activities that distinguished Simeon from other men. We do know he was "righteous," which would describe his relationship with others, and he was "devout," which describes his relationship with God.

It is often assumed Simeon was old, but if we look at the account carefully, Luke did no tell us that for sure. We don't know how long he carried God's promise that he would see the Messiah. All we know is that the Spirit revealed something to him, which Simeon accepted in faith and then waited to see its fulfillment.

Jerusalem was a busy city with lots of activity, especially around the Temple. It would have been easy for Simeon to miss his encounter with Jesus. Jesus would not have been in the Temple with His parents for very long and Simeon could have been in the general vicinity but still missed Him, except that the Spirit was ordering his steps. We see from this that Simeon was sensitive to the Spirit or perhaps the Spirit had done such a deep work in his life that he had a thought that he needed to be somewhere and followed that thought in faith.

## The Implications

There seem to be two pictures that people hold in their minds when we say someone is in the Spirit. We either think of a wide-eyed, eccentric person who walks around with his (or her) head cocked to one side, listening for a voice that no one else can hear. Or there is the person who only does what "the Spirit" tells him (or her) to do, and thus takes no initiative on his (or her) own unless God speaks. I am not sure either of those would adequately describe Simeon. Paul is the one who gave us the best picture for what someone in the Spirit is like:

> Those who live according to the flesh have their minds set on what the flesh desires; but those who live in accordance with the Spirit have their minds set on what the Spirit desires. The mind governed by the flesh is death, but the mind governed by the Spirit is life and peace. The mind governed by the flesh is hostile to God; it does not submit to God's law, nor can it do so. Those who are in the realm of the flesh cannot please God. You, however, are not in the realm of the flesh but are in the realm of the Spirit, if indeed the Spirit of God lives in you. And if anyone does not have the Spirit of Christ, they do not belong to Christ. But if Christ is in you, then even though your body is subject to death because of sin, the Spirit gives life because of righteousness. And if the Spirit of him who raised Jesus from the dead is living in you, he who raised Christ from the dead will also give life to your mortal bodies because of his Spirit who lives in you (Romans 8:5-11).

It seems that the presence of the Spirit is most active in the area of our minds, and the business of our minds is thinking. Therefore, those who are in the Spirit are those whose thought processes and eventual thoughts themselves are subject to the work of the Spirit. A Proverbs 31 man is one whose mind is not set on sports, business, gambling, sex, or trivial or wasteful hobbies. The Proverbs 31 man's mind is not hostile to God or His will but submits to God's will as revealed in His word and through His Spirit. There is an abundance of instruction in the epistles that describes the behavior and thinking of a man led by the Spirit. Perhaps it would be a good study to look at what those writers had to say as a follow up to this chapter.

If the mind governed by the flesh is death, then the mind ruled by the Spirit is life and that life is contagious and should be shared with others. That means men who are in the Spirit are teaching and encouraging others, just like Simeon did with Joseph, Mary, and Jesus in the Temple.

Are you a man (or woman) of the Spirit? If so, you don't have to follow the expectations of those who think you must be spooky spiritual if you have a close relationship with the Spirit. You can be supernaturally natural and still be a man or person of the Spirit. I encourage you to reflect on this concept and see if your mind is indeed a source of life for others, or a source of contention or useless pursuits that don't amount to anything in the eternal economy of God.

# CHAPTER 8

## Another Joseph

There are a few men named Joseph described in biblical narratives. One is the Old Testament Joseph of Genesis fame. Then there is Joseph, the father of Jesus (who we will look at later), and also Joseph in Acts 4 who was given the nickname Barnabas. There is one other Joseph I want to focus on in this chapter and that is Joseph of Arimathea. Remember, the characteristics of a Proverbs 31 man we are looking for are:

1. Using leadership power to benefit and not harm those who are weaker.
2. Being concerned for social justice.
3. Honoring women.
4. Serving in leadership capacities as "elders at the gate," where wisdom and justice are dispensed.

My goal is to stir up modern men to take their place alongside the Proverbs 31 men in the Bible. Based on my experience in my church and from my travels, this is not happening.

**Who Was This Man?**

I found four references to Joseph of Arimathea:

1. **He was a disciple and follower of Jesus.** "When evening came, a rich man from Arimathea named Joseph, one of Jesus' followers, went to Pilate and asked for Jesus' body. And Pilate issued an order to release it to him. Joseph took the body and wrapped it in a clean linen cloth, and placed it in his own new rock-hewn tomb, and rolled a great stone across the entrance as he left" (Matthew 27:57-60).
2. **He was a bold man who was looking for God's kingdom.** "It was Preparation Day (that is, the day before the Sabbath). So as evening approached, Joseph of Arimathea, a prominent member of the Council, who was himself waiting for the kingdom of God, went boldly to Pilate and asked for Jesus' body. Pilate was surprised to hear that he was already dead. Summoning the centurion, he asked him if Jesus had already died. When he learned from the centurion that it was so, he gave the body to Joseph. So Joseph bought some linen cloth, took down the body, wrapped it in the linen, and placed it in a tomb cut out of rock. Then he rolled a stone against the entrance of the tomb" (Mark 15:42-26).
3. **He had not consented to how the Council had treated Jesus.** "Now there was a man named Joseph, a member of the Council, a good and upright man, who had not consented to their decision and action. He came from the Judean town of Arimathea, and he himself was waiting for the kingdom of God. Going to Pilate, he asked for Jesus' body. Then he took it down, wrapped it in linen cloth and placed it in a tomb cut in the rock, one in which no one

had yet been laid. It was Preparation Day, and the Sabbath was about to begin. The women who had come with Jesus from Galilee followed Joseph and saw the tomb and how his body was laid in it. Then they went home and prepared spices and perfumes. But they rested on the Sabbath in obedience to the commandment" (Luke 23:50-56).

4. **Even though bold, Joseph was a secret disciple because he feared the Jewish leaders.** "Later, Joseph of Arimathea asked Pilate for the body of Jesus. Now Joseph was a disciple of Jesus, but secretly because he feared the Jewish leaders. With Pilate's permission, he came and took the body away. He was accompanied by Nicodemus, the man who earlier had visited Jesus at night. Nicodemus brought a mixture of myrrh and aloes, about seventy-five pounds. Taking Jesus' body, the two of them wrapped it, with the spices, in strips of linen. This was in accordance with Jewish burial customs. At the place where Jesus was crucified, there was a garden, and in the garden a new tomb, in which no one had ever been laid. Because it was the Jewish day of Preparation and since the tomb was nearby, they laid Jesus there" (John 19:38-42).

### What Can We Learn from Him?

Here are some things about Joseph that stand out and are capable of helping us become a Proverbs 31 man (or woman).

1. He was not a perfect man, for he was a secret disciple because he feared the backlash of his culture. God still used him and honored him by telling his story in all four gospels.

2. Jesus' death, rather than causing him to shrink deeper into fear, caused him to come out and identify with the dead Jesus.
3. He was not primarily a Jewish man or a synagogue man. His loyalty was not ultimately to his people or his "church," but to the Kingdom of God.
4. His courage inspired Nicodemus, who we must also assume was a "secret" disciple.
5. The women followed Joseph to learn what he had done and where Jesus was so they could follow up with their own devotion to the dead Jesus when the Sabbath was over.
6. Joseph used his wealth to help the poor, for he gave his expensive tomb to a man who could not pay him for it. Anyone familiar with Jewish culture knows how important a burial is for a Jew.
7. While Joseph was a secret disciple, he publicly disagreed with the mistreatment of Jesus and the unjust sentence of the Council.

Here are some questions to ask yourself in light of what we just read and learned. **Where is fear keeping you a "secret" disciple of Jesus? Are you bound by your wealth or love of money? Are you bold for the cause of Christ? Are you more committed to your church or your race than you are to the Kingdom and its values?**

**Do women follow your leadership? Are you impacting others to be bold in their faith? Do you have the courage to speak up to disagree with less-than-godly decisions made at work, in your church, or in your family?** I pray God will grant you the grace to answer these questions honestly and then give more to the Kingdom and its cause than to any other voice that is vying for your attention.

# CHAPTER 9

## The Tax Man

There was no more hated group of Jewish citizens in Jesus' day than the tax collectors. These men were employed by Herod to collect taxes for Rome and for Herod's projects, and anything "left over" belonged to the collectors. These men had a franchise that empowered them to legally loot their own people and thus the reason for the animosity toward them. The Jews could think of no greater insult to hurl at Jesus than this: "Here is a glutton and a drunkard, a friend of tax collectors and sinners" (Luke 7:34). It is not surprising then that Jesus would call one of those men to become a disciple and also a good example of a Proverbs 31 man, the subject of this book and study.

### The Call

Jesus' ministry was based in the region of Galilee by the large lake where some of His disciples made their living as fishermen. Levi was there to collect business taxes from those men, but then one day Jesus walked by and this is what happened: "After this, Jesus went out and saw a tax collector by the name of Levi sitting at his tax booth. 'Follow me,' Jesus said to him, and Levi got up, left everything and followed him" (Luke 5:27:28). My theory is that this was not the first encounter between these two men. Perhaps Levi and Jesus had previously conversed or maybe Levi had witnessed Jesus' public ministry.

That being said, when Levi heard the call, he abandoned his lucrative occupation and followed Jesus. After that, whenever the apostles were named, Levi was included but was identified by his other name of Matthew:

> When morning came, he called his disciples to him and chose twelve of them, whom he also designated apostles: Simon (whom he named Peter), his brother Andrew, James, John, Philip, Bartholomew, Matthew, Thomas, James son of Alphaeus, Simon who was called the Zealot, Judas son of James, and Judas Iscariot, who became a traitor (Luke 6:13-16).

Matthew abandoned his wealth and source of revenue to follow and fellowship with Jesus. The reason I believe Matthew was acquainted with Jesus is because of what Matthew did after he began following Jesus: "Then Levi held a great banquet for Jesus at his house, and a large crowd of tax collectors and others were eating with them" (Luke 5:29). Matthew knew Jesus' mission was to reach people just like he was, so he used his connections to spread the word and give his peers the same chance he had to encounter and learn from Jesus of Nazareth.

## The Lessons for Us

Levi had been rejected by the scribes of his day, but Jesus chose him to be His scribe. Matthew went on to write a gospel directed toward his people the Jews, explaining and proving that Jesus was their Messiah. Matthew displayed two of the four traits of a Proverbs 31 man: 1) using leadership power to benefit and not harm those who are weaker; and 2) serving in a leadership capacity as an elder at the gate where he could dispense wisdom and justice.

To become a Proverbs 31 man, Levi had to display courage and walk away from his occupation. He had to embrace his past, be forgiven, and then bear fruit consistent with his new life. Because he did, he is still serving the Lord and blessing the people of God though his writing and teaching.

Is Jesus calling you to be a Proverbs 31 man? It may not be necessary to walk away from your work, but then again, it may. If that is what He is asking you to do, you will not do it alone, for He is calling you to walk with Him so that together you may redefine your role, not according to what others think, but according to His purpose and plan for you. I urge you not to let anything—money, occupation, sports, relationships, or fear—keep you from being a Proverbs 31 man who is able to accept a new role not only as a breadwinner for your family but also a soul winner for Christ.

# CHAPTER 10

## Powerful in the Word

In our search for what I term Proverbs 31 men in the Bible, we have looked so far at Mordecai, Amos, Onesiphorus, Ezra, and Matthew. The qualities necessary for a man to be labeled as such are one or more of the following traits as found in Proverbs 31:

1. Using leadership power to benefit and not harm those who are weaker.
2. Being concerned for social justice.
3. Honoring women.
4. Serving in leadership capacities as "elders at the gate," where wisdom and justice are dispensed.

In this chapter, let's look at a man named Apollos, who is prominently mentioned in the books of Acts seven times and once in Paul's first letter to the Corinthians.

### Who Was This Man?

We are first introduced to Apollos in Acts 18:24: "Meanwhile a Jew named Apollos, a native of Alexandria, came to Ephesus. He was a learned man, with a thorough knowledge of the Scriptures." If there is one designation I would covet in my career, it would be as a man who was *competent in the Scriptures* as another translation put it. Apollos was a Jew from Egypt, a center of Jewish learning and Greek culture, and he was a traveling teacher, not an uncommon thing in his day: "He had been instructed in the way of the Lord, and he spoke with great fervor and taught about Jesus accurately, though he knew only the baptism of John. He began to speak boldly in the synagogue" (Acts 18:25-26a).

The problem was that what Apollos taught was accurate but incomplete, which was sort of like taking algebra one, which is true and complete, but is not the full picture without algebra two. Apollos had only heard about John's baptism, so he was probably preaching a message of repentance and heart preparation for the coming of the Messiah.

Luke then tell us that "when Priscilla and Aquila heard him, they invited him to their home and explained to him the way of God more adequately" (Acts 18:26b). Apollos humbled himself and received the missing pieces of his message, which he obviously accepted eagerly and with gladness, for Paul did not hesitate to endorse and draw on Apollos' ministry assistance: "I planted the seed, Apollos watered it, but God has been making it grow" (1 Corinthians 3:6).

## Proverbs 31 Qualifications

What qualified Apollos to be considered a Proverbs 31 man for the purposes of this study? First and foremost, he made his teaching gift available to the body of Christ, free of charge:

> When Apollos wanted to go to Achaia, the brothers and sisters encouraged him and wrote to the disciples there to welcome him. When he arrived, he was a great help to those who by grace had believed. For he vigorously refuted his Jewish opponents in public debate, proving from the Scriptures that Jesus was the Messiah (Acts 18:27-28).

Apollos served as an elder at the gate, so to speak, and made his wisdom accessible to build up his listeners. There are some who think he contributed to or perhaps even wrote the letter to the Hebrews. He used his leadership power, which derived from the exercise of his teaching gift and his years of studying God's word, to empower others in the knowledge of God's purpose in Christ. I could even make a case that he honored women, for he received instruction from both Aquilla *and* Priscilla, and most credit Priscilla with the more prominent ministry of the two because her name is usually mentioned first.

You don't have to be a great teacher like Apollos, or have a public ministry at all, to be considered a modern Proverbs 31 man. What will qualify you is recognizing your spiritual gifts, perfecting them through use and practice, and then making them available to bless as many people as possible. What's more, Apollos didn't seem like he waited for an invitation to go somewhere; he usually just went! A Proverbs 31 man doesn't wait to be invited to serve or bless, so when he sees a need and has the ability to address it, he does so. Of course, the same is true for Proverbs 31 women.

Where have you been holding back your gift and presence in the church or society? Where have you allowed fear or misplaced priorities to render God's deposit in your life ineffective? Have sports, career, or family detracted from your ability to serve? It appears Apollos lived a life of faith, trusting the Lord for his provision as he traveled and taught. Not only did God provide for his physical needs but the Lord also gave him the insight he needed to be even more effective as he served the Lord. It's time for men everywhere to stand up, declare "this is who I am and what God has equipped me to do," and then do it. The need has never been greater, but the rewards are the same: hearing the words "Well done, good and faithful service" at the end of a life devoted not to personal comfort but selfless servant.

# CHAPTER 11

## A Husband-and-Wife Team

Let's look at the male part of the most famous New Testament ministry duo: Priscilla and Aquila. This couple was obviously a dynamic team, so to separate them to determine what they did individually is almost impossible. What's more, in most cases, Priscilla's name is listed first when they are mentioned, which leads some to believe that she was the more gifted of the two for ministry. If that's the case, God saw fit to join her to a Proverbs 31 man who would protect, nurture, and release her ministry purpose. We first encounter Aquila in Acts 18:1-3:

> After this, Paul left Athens and went to Corinth. There he met a Jew named Aquila, a native of Pontus, who had recently come from Italy with his wife Priscilla, because Claudius had ordered all Jews to leave Rome. Paul went to see them, and because he was a tentmaker as they were, he stayed and worked with them.

### Roving Hospitality

In the last chapter, we saw that Aquila and his wife

brought Apollos into their home to teach him more about the Way, and then we see that they did the same for Paul. Paul then added this bit of information in Romans 16:3-5,

> Greet Priscilla and Aquila, my co-workers in Christ Jesus. They risked their lives for me. Not only I but all the churches of the Gentiles are grateful to them. Greet also the church that meets at their house.

Once again, we see that Aquila made his home available for many and of course Priscilla was a willing accomplice. We learn from these few verses that the couple lived in Rome, Corinth, and then back in Rome again, after a journey to Syria and a stay in Ephesus:

> Paul stayed on in Corinth for some time. Then he left the brothers and sisters and sailed for Syria, accompanied by Priscilla and Aquila. Before he sailed, he had his hair cut off at Cenchreae because of a vow he had taken. They arrived at Ephesus, where Paul left Priscilla and Aquila. He himself went into the synagogue and reasoned with the Jews (Acts 18:18-19).

Not only did the couple offer hospitality by opening their home to God's people, they also moved their home to wherever God needed them to be. Then they made themselves useful wherever they were. At some point, their service to Paul put their own lives in danger but they willingly volunteered for duty even though danger was involved.

It also seems that this couple had a knack to recognize "talent," if that is the right word, for they allied themselves first with Paul and then Apollos to help those men become more effective at what God had called them to do.

### The Qualifications

I have defined a Proverbs 31 man as someone who does one or all of the following:

1. Using leadership power to benefit and not harm

those who are weaker.

2. Being concerned for social justice.
3. Honoring women.
4. Serving in leadership capacities as "elders at the gate," where wisdom and justice are dispensed.

How does Aquila qualify? Of course, he honored his wife by being willing as a Jewish man to partner with her in ministry, even giving her preeminence according to the Spirit's will. He also served as an elder at the gate of the Church, but that "gate" moved from city to city. Aquila did not need a title, a physical office, or a job description. He simply needed an opportunity to serve and he made himself useful according to the needs of the moment. He also used his leadership power to empower others, first Paul, then Apollos, and finally those who were in his house church.

My goal in this book is to stir up more men to be involved in society and the church through finding and fulfilling their purpose. I want to see them as passionate for the Lord as they are for sports, career, and earning a living. Aquila was a man whose household was sold out for the Lord. His wife was not the more spiritual of the two even if she was the more gifted. Aquila contributed what he could and was devoted to the cause of the Kingdom, so much so that he risked his life and sacrificed his career to be God's agent. He was not concerned about building up equity in a house; he was interested in building up equity in heaven through practical service. May more men catch the spirit and vision of Aquila and may they use all at their disposal to serve the saints and the Kingdom as God directs.

# CHAPTER 12

## Going to Samaria

We have been studying examples from the Bible of what I am referring to as Proverbs 31 men, who meet one or more of these criteria:

1. Using leadership power to benefit and not harm those who are weaker.
2. Being concerned for social justice.
3. Honoring women.
4. Serving in leadership capacities as "elders at the gate," where wisdom and justice are dispensed.

In this chapter, let's look at a man named Philip who has an entire chapter devoted to his work in Acts. We first meet Philip in Acts 6:5 when the church elected its first deacons: "This proposal pleased the whole group. They chose Stephen, a man full of faith and of the Holy Spirit; also Philip, Procorus, Nicanor, Timon, Parmenas, and Nicolas from Antioch, a convert to Judaism." We learn from this verse that others recognized the presence of the Spirit in his life that manifested in wisdom for the benefit of others. What else do we know about this man that qualifies him to be a Proverbs 31 man?

## Wisdom and the Spirit

The next time we read about Philip is in Acts 8:

> Those who had been scattered preached the word wherever they went. Philip went down to a city in Samaria and proclaimed the Messiah there. When the crowds heard Philip and saw the signs he performed, they all paid close attention to what he said. For with shrieks, impure spirits came out of many, and many who were paralyzed or lame were healed. So there was great joy in that city (Acts 8:4-8).

Once again, Philip endeared himself to others by serving their needs in the power of the Spirit and the practicality of his wisdom. He had the foresight to go to Samaria after the persecution caused by Stephen's death, and he had the people's undivided attention as he addressed their spiritual and physical needs. The result was great joy in the city. That's what I want my legacy to be that people were helped and healed when I came around, which resulted in great rejoicing in the Lord. However, that's not all Philip did, for he is perhaps best known for the next encounter he had with an Ethiopian eunuch:

> Now an angel of the Lord said to Philip, "Go south to the road—the desert road—that goes down from Jerusalem to Gaza." So he started out, and on his way he met an Ethiopian eunuch, an important official in charge of all the treasury of the Kandake (which means "queen of the Ethiopians"). This man had gone to Jerusalem to worship, and on his way home was sitting in his chariot reading the Book of Isaiah the prophet. The Spirit told Philip, "Go to that chariot and stay near it." Then Philip ran up to the chariot and heard the man reading Isaiah the prophet. "Do you understand what you are reading?" Philip asked (Acts 8:26-30).

Philip explained the passage from Isaiah to the eunuch

and shared "the good news about Jesus" (Acts 8:35). He baptized the eunuch, but then "the Spirit of the Lord suddenly took Philip away, and the eunuch did not see him again, but went on his way rejoicing" (Acts 8:39). Once again, Philip's presence was the source of great joy for someone else. We are told from there, Philip "traveled about, preaching the gospel in all the towns until he reached Caesarea" (Acts 8:40b). Then Philip disappears from Acts until much later when we learn what is perhaps his most important role that qualified him as a Proverbs 31 man.

### What Else?

Luke reported in Acts 21:8-9, "Leaving the next day, we reached Caesarea and stayed at the house of Philip the evangelist, one of the Seven. He had four unmarried daughters who prophesied." We read in Acts 8 that Philip went to Caesarea and in Acts 21 we find out what he was doing there: evangelizing and raising four girls who followed in their father's footsteps by being full of the Spirit and wisdom. They spoke the words of God and we can be sure they brought joy to the hearts of others just like their father had done on numerous occasions. Philip raised four women who served as prophetic voices, which eventually brought them into the presence of Luke and the Apostle Paul.

Philip was a Proverbs 31 man who met all four criteria we find in Proverbs 31 as described above. He was a servant leader extraordinaire who met the needs of many people, helped introduce Christianity in Ethiopia, and honored the equality of women in the things of God. Good things happened to others no matter where Philip went.

We need more men like Philip in the church today who devote their lives not to entertainment or frivolous issues but rather to the distribution of wisdom and joy in the power of the Holy Spirit. I want to follow in Philip's footsteps, and I invite my brothers to join me so we can impact our generation like Philip did his.

# CHAPTER 13

## Sons of Thunder 1

As we continue our search for examples of what I am referring to as Proverbs 31 men, in the next two chapters, I want to consider two brothers, James and John, starting with John. I could write much about John, especially if we assume that he wrote the epistles and the three letters of John, but I am going to focus on John in the gospels. Don't confuse John the disciple and apostle of Jesus with John the Baptist who was Jesus' cousin. This John's mother's name was Salome, and she will figure into our discussion in the next chapter when we look at James, so let's get started with John.

### The Background

John was a fisherman, as was his brother and father:

> Going on from there, he saw two other brothers, James son of Zebedee and his brother John. They were in a boat with their father Zebedee, preparing their nets. Jesus called them, and immediately they left the boat and their father and followed him (Matthew 4:21-22).

Soon thereafter, Jesus gave the brothers a nickname: "James son of Zebedee and his brother John (to them he gave the name Boanerges, which means "sons of thunder")" (Mark 3:17). Some believe Jesus gave them this nickname because of their thunderous temper; others maintain it is because they were more like "sons of windbags," making a lot of noise but not always producing the lightning. It could have been a combination of both: anger causing them to speak before they thought through what was said.

In Mark 9, we see John was upset that someone was doing good deeds, even though they were not among their apostolic band of brothers: "'Teacher,' said John, 'we saw someone driving out demons in your name and we told him to stop, because he was not one of us'" (Mark 9:38). Later, John suggested that unfriendly fire consume those who had insulted Jesus and His team:

> And he sent messengers on ahead, who went into a Samaritan village to get things ready for him; but the people there did not welcome him, because he was heading for Jerusalem. When the disciples James and John saw this, they asked, "Lord, do you want us to call fire down from heaven to destroy them?" But Jesus turned and rebuked them (Luke 9:52-55).

Let's summarize: John had an anger problem that caused him to lash out when wronged and seek revenge on his enemies, especially the Samaritans, who he despised like all good Jews were taught to do.

## The Transformation

In Luke 9, we saw that John was ready to nuke the Samaritans. Then we read this extraordinary account of John's ministry work in Acts:

> When the apostles in Jerusalem heard that Samaria had accepted the word of God, they sent Peter and John to Samaria. When they arrived, they prayed

> for the new believers there that they might receive the Holy Spirit, because the Holy Spirit had not yet come on any of them; they had simply been baptized in the name of the Lord Jesus. Then Peter and John placed their hands on them, and they received the Holy Spirit (Acts 9:14-17).

Not only did John go to Samaria, he laid his hands on the Samaritans! That is a remarkable transformation. After that encounter, Luke wrote, "After they had further proclaimed the word of the Lord and testified about Jesus, Peter and John returned to Jerusalem, preaching the gospel in many Samaritan villages" (Acts 9:25). John overcame his prejudice and anger to become an apostle, no longer representing his own feelings and opinions, but representing the Lord in the power of His Spirit. John not only went to the Samaritans, he also made physical contact with them.

The Church needs more Proverbs 31 men like John who are more committed to the Kingdom than to their race, culture, or political party. We need more Proverbs 31 men who, like John, have an encounter with the Spirit that allows them to be sent to where the Spirit is working and moving, even if it is to a culture they previously hated or avoided. We need men who are not just thunderous windbags or blowhards, but who can lay hands on others and see God touch them. We need more Proverbs 31 men who will own up to their anger, apologize for where and to whom it did harm, and then direct their passion not toward sports, business, or trivial things but to the matters of God's Kingdom.

If John could transform so dramatically, then we can, too—and that includes men *and* women. In the next chapter, we will look at the other brother, but for now, I urge you to face your own limitations, yield them to the Spirt for Him to transform, and then become a Proverbs 31 man who can seek justice for all and not just those in his own little world of like-minded or like-looking people.

# CHAPTER 14

## Sons of Thunder 2

In the last chapter, we looked at the Apostle John and now we will look at his brother, James, both of whom Jesus nicknamed the sons of thunder (see Mark 3:17). These brothers were Simon's business partners (see Luke 5:10) in the fishing industry and lived in the area of Galilee. I am profiling them because they are Proverbs 31 men and fulfilled one or more of the characteristics found in Proverbs 31:

1. Using leadership power to benefit and not harm those who are weaker.
2. Being concerned for social justice.
3. Honoring women.
4. Serving in leadership capacities as "elders at the gate," where wisdom and justice are dispensed.

Let's get started.

### The Mother

Some have conjectured that the sons-of-thunder reference was not concerning the brothers but their mother, whom some believe was a woman named Salome who was often part of Jesus' traveling entourage (see Mark 15:40-41 and Mark 16:1). Others maintain that Salome was Mary's sister, which would have made her Jesus' aunt and the brothers His cousins. Whoever this woman was and whatever her relationship was to Jesus, she came to him with a "thunderously" bold request:

> Then the mother of Zebedee's sons came to Jesus with her sons and, kneeling down, asked a favor of him. "What is it you want?" he asked. She said, "Grant that one of these two sons of mine may sit at your right and the other at your left in your kingdom." "You don't know what you are asking," Jesus said to them. "Can you drink the cup I am going to drink?" "We can," they answered. Jesus said to them, "You will indeed drink from my cup, but to sit at my right or left is not for me to grant. These places belong to those for whom they have been prepared by my Father" (Matthew 20:20-23).

Her boys were right next to Salome, kneeling before Jesus, as they attempted to undercut the others and secure a special seat in the Kingdom as they understood it. Jesus did not honor the request, but He did ask the brothers a question, which they answered without realizing the scope or implications of their response. He asked if they could drink from His cup, which they said they could. Perhaps they thought the cup was some kind of inconvenience or annoyance. Instead, it was their cross that they would be required to pick up daily as they followed Jesus. Those brothers could and did indeed drink the cup but when they answered, they had not a clue as to its contents.

In a sense, Jesus did grant the request of this bold woman, for both her sons went on to play an important role in Jesus' Kingdom, one for a long time but the other for much shorter than what anyone, including either brother, would have expected. Let's look at what happened to James and you will see what I mean.

## A Timely Death

Jesus took James with Him as one of His most trusted disciples at critical times, like His transfiguration, the raising of a dead girl, and His time of prayer in the Garden before His betrayal. It would seem that James was heading for a significant earthly role in the Kingdom of God, until we read what happened in Acts 12:1-2: "It was about this time that King Herod arrested some who belonged to the church, intending to persecute them. He had James, the brother of John, put to death with the sword." James did drink the cup to which Jesus referred by dying a martyr's death, the first death of an apostle who stayed loyal to Jesus (I won't count Judas' death). By the way, the Herod who killed James was the nephew of the Herod who had killed John the Baptist.

James' brother John by all accounts lived many more years in faithful service to Jesus, but it would seem that James went home to glory quite early—or least earlier than we would have expected due to His time spent in Jesus' inner circle. His death undoubtedly shook up the apostolic party who had delayed obeying Jesus' command to go by staying in Jerusalem for a few years after Jesus' Ascension. With James killed, the men knew their own days were numbered and tradition tells us that one by one, they all went out and fulfilled Matthew 28:19-20, all but John, his brother, joining James as martyrs.

You may ask, "How does that qualify James to be a Proverbs 31 man?" My response is that Herod knew exactly where to find James because he was accessible and available in Galilee as a leader in the church, serving the Lord's people. James did not use his special status and favor with Jesus to build his own kingdom or establish his own power base, but used it as a means to serve the Lord and His cause. James' death served as an incentive for his band of brothers to get up and get going.

Jesus is still seeking men (and women) who will put aside their own ambitions, as James and John did, to serve His purpose in their generation. He is recruiting men who will drink the cup and suffer, flying against the wind of their culture that says they are real men only if they love sports, gambling, leisure, and personal hobbies. I am hoping to stir up and mobilize a cadre of Proverbs 31 men who will serve the Lord and His people in this day when men have shied away from the Church, finding other interests to occupy their time and energy. May the Spirit of the sons of thunder come upon us all, and may we drink from the cup and yield our lives to spread and establish His kingdom on earth.

# CHAPTER 15

## A Good Writer

In this chapter, we look at a Proverbs 31 man whose name is only mentioned three times (maybe four) in the New Testament, but his literary fingerprints are found throughout. His name is Luke, the "dear friend and doctor" (Colossians 4:14), whose two books named *Luke* and *Acts* provide insight into the life of Jesus and the early church that no one could have provided like Luke did.

Luke is the only Gentile writer in the Bible. Being a doctor who wrote with the best Greek style due to his education, Luke provided an orderly account, conducting extensive research and interviews for his gospel accounts. Luke's first gospel was written for a Gentile audience and highlighted Jesus' treatment of and care for women, something the Jewish writers would have been less apt to emphasize. Luke also gave us a firsthand account in much of Acts, as signified by his use of the first-person plural pronoun *we*, which means he would often have been the companion of the Apostle Paul. Let's look at what else we can learn about Luke that is applicable to our pursuit of principles to help us qualify as Proverbs 31 men (or women) in our generation.

## Who Was This Man?

We don't know much more about Luke except that he was probably mentioned in Acts 13:1, "Now in the church at Antioch there were prophets and teachers: Barnabas, Simeon called Niger, **Lucius of Cyrene**, Manaen (who had been brought up with Herod the tetrarch) and Saul." If Luke is indeed the same man as Lucius in this verse, then he was present at the start of Saul's call to missions work among the Gentiles. Who better to later accompany Paul on his journeys than the man who was there and heard the Spirit's voice call Saul into such a mission?

Keep in mind that Saul's ministry was always viewed with some suspicion by the leaders in Jerusalem. What's more, when believing Jews heard about Paul's teaching among the Gentiles, they fed the suspicion as we learn from Luke's report in Acts 21:20b-22:

> Then they said to Paul: "You see, brother, how many thousands of Jews have believed, and all of them are zealous for the law. They have been informed that you teach all the Jews who live among the Gentiles to turn away from Moses, telling them not to circumcise their children or live according to our customs."

It would make sense that Luke began traveling with Paul as first reported in Acts 16:10 to bear witness to and record the validity and importance of Paul's mission to those who questioned it. Luke's testimony would have verified the Spirit's presence in Paul's ministry work and addressed the concerns of Jerusalem, who would have had a closer relationship with Barnabas and John Mark—both of whom had to part ways with Paul when they tried to work together. Yet there was perhaps an even more important role Luke played in helping take the gospel to his own people, the Gentiles, and that was he became Paul's friend.

## Closer than a Brother

Paul reported in 2 Timothy 4:11 that "only Luke is with

me. Get Mark and bring him with you, because he is helpful to me in my ministry." Luke became friends with a man who was not easy to be friends with (ask Barnabas or Mark). Luke traveled with Paul, sometimes as his only companion, and probably helped him with practical things, always keeping an accurate journal so he could also tend to his literary calling. When Paul was imprisoned in Caesarea for two years before he went to Rome, Luke undoubtedly visited him in prison while he also conducted his research for his gospel. Then when Paul went to Rome, Luke wrote,

> When it was decided that we would sail for Italy, Paul and some other prisoners were handed over to a centurion named Julius, who belonged to the Imperial Regiment. *We* boarded a ship from Adramyttium about to sail for ports along the coast of the province of Asia, and we put out to sea. Aristarchus, a Macedonian from Thessalonica, was with us (Acts 27:1-2, emphasis added).

Luke traveled the world with Paul and ended up on the ill-fated ship that ran aground on its way to Rome. He had to make it to shore like everyone else, finding something that would help him float as he swam to safety. Like Paul, Luke's life was in danger, all to fulfill Proverbs 18:24: "One who has unreliable friends soon comes to ruin, *but there is a friend who sticks closer than a brother*" (emphasis added). When Paul lived in Rome in rented quarters for two years, in all probability Luke was there with him.

Luke was a Proverbs 31 man, for he ensured that Jerusalem and then posterity would recognize and honor the importance of Paul's work. Luke could have been a "local elder" but instead he became a "floating" assistant whose office as pastor was carried out as a writer and historian. Luke submitted his intelligence, education, and calling to the service of one man and one cause, and God has honored him with a place among the heroes of the faith, almost all of whom were

Jewish—except for Luke, the beloved physician. May we all, men and women, submit our lives to the service of God and others as Luke did, and may God grant us the strength to see that commitment through to the end, for His glory and the good of his church.

# CHAPTER 16

## An Egyptian

Next up is a man who I consider to be one of the finest leaders in the Bible. He was not a Jew, part of the covenant/faith community, or someone who knew the Bible or wrote a psalm. He was the leader of Egypt, given the title Pharaoh, but he was not the Pharaoh who probably first comes to your mind. He was not the Pharaoh of Moses; he was the Pharaoh of Joseph. How can I make such a bold claim that he was one of the best? Read on and then see if you agree with me that this Pharaoh was indeed a great leader and also a Proverbs 31 man.

### Some History

Egypt in Joseph's times was the most powerful nation in the world. When Joseph first arrived, Egypt prospered under Pharaoh's leadership and there was no end in sight of their power or wealth. While Joseph was imprisoned, a drama played out that started with Pharaoh's famous doubleheader dreams. Joseph helped Pharaoh understand the dreams and what the nation needed to do to prepare for a coming world-wide famine. The period leading up to the dream, the dream interpretation, and the dream application all give us valuable lessons from Pharaoh's leadership that we would do well to emulate. We will see that he embodied a few of the characteristics of a Proverbs 31 man, which include:

1. Using leadership power to benefit and not harm those who are weaker.
2. Being concerned for social justice.
3. Honoring women.
4. Serving in leadership capacities as "elders at the gate," where wisdom and justice are dispensed.

Pharaoh met the qualifications for three of those four traits. Let' see how he did it.

## The Qualifications

Here are the reasons I make the claim that Pharaoh was a great leader and Proverbs 31 man.

1. Pharaoh used his power not to build his own kingdom but to serve those who were weaker and not in a position to help themselves. Joseph was a man with a shady past and a prison record, but Pharaoh saw wisdom and potential in the young man, so he promoted him. When you think of it, he also promoted the man who eventually introduced him to Joseph for Pharaoh restored his butler and "fired" his baker after they were placed on "probation." Pharaoh's objective all along was to care for his people, not to concentrate all his power into one super-Pharaoh position.
2. Pharaoh saw the need and the opportunity to prepare for the coming famine so he exalted Joseph to a high position so food could be stored for the people. Yes, eventually Pharaoh bartered food for land and ended up owning all

the land, but the people were willing partners in the process. He provided for their needs, including the needs of Joseph, who received power, honor, a wife, and a place for his family during the famine. Pharaoh knew how to treat those on his staff and he was concerned with justice by ensuring that all his people could be fed—not just the rich.

3. Pharaoh concluded that he did not have the vision for the future and was not threatened to give Joseph a high position with all the authority he needed to carry out the plenty-to-famine plan. Pharaoh was secure in who he was and served as an elder at the gate of his society and culture, and his strategy was to let go and let Joseph. The results were astounding, for not only did the plan save Egypt, it saved the entire population around Egypt that came to buy food. What's more, God used those circumstances to relocate His people to Egypt of their own free will, thus providing a good example of God's sovereignty operating in the context of man's freedom to choose.

If you want to read more about Joseph's Pharaoh, you can access an article I wrote on my website titled *Leadership Lessons from Egypt*. As you read, I hope you will not only be convinced that my claim of his superb leadership is accurate, but that also you will set a goal to be like him whether you are a man or women, leader or future leader, person with a title or only a vision for the future. This book is titled *Proverbs 31 Men*, so I do hope my male readers will take these lessons to heart and follow in the steps of one of the Bible's truly great leaders, Joseph's Pharaoh.

# CHAPTER 17

## A True Son

I have heard the subject of spiritual sons and fathers discussed in some churches where much is made of the "father of the house" and "spiritual sons." At times, the concept has become trivialized when it is carried to extreme ends, but that is not what I want to write about in this chapter. Instead, I want to look at Paul's spiritual son, Timothy, and see if Timothy qualifies as a Proverbs 31 man, the theme of this book. Let's start by reading what Paul wrote in Philippians 2:19-23:

> I hope in the Lord Jesus to send Timothy to you soon, that I also may be cheered when I receive news about you. I have no one else like him, who will show genuine concern for your welfare. For everyone looks out for their own interests, not those of Jesus Christ. But you know that Timothy has proved himself, because as a son with his father he has served with me in the work of the gospel. I hope, therefore, to send him as soon as I see how things go with me.

What can we learn about Timothy from this passage?

## What Price Leadership?

Before we answer that question, let's look at the story of how Paul and Timothy met:

> Paul came to Derbe and then to Lystra, where a disciple named Timothy lived, whose mother was Jewish and a believer but whose father was a Greek. The believers at Lystra and Iconium spoke well of him. Paul wanted to take him along on the journey, so he circumcised him because of the Jews who lived in that area, for they all knew that his father was a Greek. As they traveled from town to town, they delivered the decisions reached by the apostles and elders in Jerusalem for the people to obey. So the churches were strengthened in the faith and grew daily in numbers (Acts 16:1-5).

Notice how Timothy got started in ministry. He did not attend seminary or go through a discipleship program. He did not have to prove himself before Paul would admit him to his inner circle. What was the requirement for Timothy to work with Paul? He had to be circumcised! We won't debate why Paul thought it important for Timothy to have this procedure performed but consider the impact of the decision. It was certainly painful and probably a bit humbling to submit to the process of one man making a slight alteration to another man's most private and sensitive part of his anatomy.

Yet Timothy must have realized it was not about him and his comfort or about his position as a number two man to Paul. It was about Paul's mission. Timothy didn't get to carry Paul's Bible or tend to his personal needs (although he probably did that at other times) as his entry point to ministry. Timothy had to mark his manhood with a sign of submission to God and then Paul considered him ready for a life of service. For that reason, I almost assigned this chapter the title "Ouch."

## His Credentials

Today when we look at Philippians 2, we see the outcome of Timothy's submission to the circumciser's knife. Paul wrote that he had no one else like Timothy. That is a remarkable statement, considering that Paul traveled with the likes of Silas, Barnabas, Luke, Mark, Titus, and others. What set Timothy apart from those men? His preaching? His spiritual gifts? His charisma? No, it was none of those things. It was his absence of self that allowed him to be genuinely concerned for others' interests, even when they conflicted with his own:

> I hope in the Lord Jesus to send Timothy to you soon, that I also may be cheered when I receive news about you. I have no one else like him, who will show genuine concern for your welfare. For everyone looks out for their own interests, not those of Jesus Christ. But you know that Timothy has proved himself, because as a son with his father he has served with me in the work of the gospel. I hope, therefore, to send him as soon as I see how things go with me (Philippians 2:19-23).

The description of Timothy in Philippians has regularly challenged me to ask two questions. One is if Paul only saw one man who was able to move past self-interest to others-interest, then how many can I expect to see with that ability in my life? The second is much more important: Can I be the one that people meet who will summarize my existence by genuine concern for their welfare?

Being a "Timothy" isn't about being close to the man of God. It is about using that unique position to serve others. On that basis alone, Timothy qualifies as a Proverbs 31 man. It is no accident, therefore, that Paul gave his most detailed instructions about the care of widows to his trusted associate in 1 Timothy 5:1-16, thus showing that Timothy used his closeness to Paul not as a means for personal gain but to serve others—in this case, the widows.

May a generation of men like Timothy, whose manhood

has been marked by the circumcision of service, rise up in the Church today to serve the poor, the weak, and the distressed as God would have them do. Then they will be true sons not only of the fathers who trained them in ministry but also of the Father who called them into service in the first place.

# CHAPTER 18

## A Stake in the Ground

As we move along in our search for Proverbs 31 men, let's look in this chapter at two men who were among 37 men identified in the Bible as David's mighty men in 2 Samuel 23:8-39. All these men were known for great exploits while serving during David's reign, but three of them were singled out for exceptional and meritorious service. Let's look at two of the three in this *chapter.*

### Mighty Warriors

Here is what we know of Eleazar and Shammah, two of three men given special notoriety among the others:

> Next to him was **Eleazar** son of Dodai the Ahohite. As one of the three mighty warriors, he was with David when they taunted the Philistines gathered at Pas Dammim for battle. Then the Israelites retreated, but Eleazar stood his ground and struck down the Philistines till his hand grew tired and froze to the sword. The Lord brought about a great victory that day. The troops returned to Eleazar, but only to strip the dead (2 Samuel 23:9-10).

> Next to him was **Shammah** son of Agee the Hararite. When the Philistines banded together at a place where there was a field full of lentils, Israel's troops fled from them. But Shammah took his stand in the middle of the field. He defended it and struck the Philistines down, and the Lord brought about a great victory (2 Samuel 23:11-12).

Both men took a stand and helped produce a great victory for Israel's army in their battle against the Philistines. It is hard to imagine two men obtaining such singlehanded results in battle, but they both stood their ground and God worked with and through them to do great, seemingly impossible things. It is reminiscent of the verse in Hebrews 11:34 that describes some of the heroes of faith: ". . . whose weakness was turned to strength; and who became powerful in battle and routed foreign armies." Perhaps that verse was written with the mighty men in mind. Often, we want the Lord to strengthen us and *then* we will consent to go into battle. Hebrews 11:34 tells us that we must first go into battle and only *then* will we realize the strength of the Lord.

Notice in the case of both men that the army had abandoned Eleazar and Shammah, leaving them to fight alone. They "retreated" and "fled" but both those men showed great courage and resolve, took a stand, and fought so long and hard that they were unable to put their weapons down when they tried, for their hands had stiffened in the grip position.

## A Stake in the Ground

I have often used the phrase "drive a stake into the ground" and had no idea of its origin. Some say it was for homesteaders who drove a stake in the ground to identify the land they were claiming. It turns out that is also seems to have been a battle strategy used by Native Americans who would tie a rope around their warriors' ankles, tie that rope to a stake, and then drive the stake in the ground. That meant the warriors fought in place and could not retreat; they were totally committed to the battle. Without the help of the rope or stake, that is exactly what Eleazar and Shammah did, and it's what more men need to do today if the Church and God's Kingdom are to have their maximum impact.

We don't know much about these two men. Were they big and strong? Did they have exceptional fighting or martial arts skills? Were they from a military family? One thing we do know is that they had courage to stand in the day of trouble and wage war on behalf of their people. We need Proverbs 31 men who will do the same today, who will take a stand in a field, holding only the sword of the Word and the Spirit, and battle for the truth of God and for those who cannot fight for themselves. Like in 2 Samuel 23, many men have retreated and fled to find comfort and distraction in leisure, sports, or other diversions, while only a few stand and fight. I want to see an army of mighty men, not macho in their approach to others or life, but confident in who they are in Christ and the power they have in Him.

It is interesting that these men were not identified until David's last words were recorded in 2 Samuel 23:1-7. These mighty men were hidden in David just like we are hidden in Christ. He is our leader and captain, and it is for Him that we take our stand. I invite everyone, men and women, to strive to become a might person in Christ, but I especially invite my brothers to join me as we courageously oppose our culture's message in order to be mighty men of God in our generation.

# CHAPTER 19

## Great Faith

To review, I have identified four attributes that qualify anyone in the Bible or today to be labeled what I am calling a Proverbs 31 man:

1. Using leadership power to benefit and not harm those who are weaker.
2. Being concerned for social justice.
3. Honoring women.
4. Serving in leadership capacities as "elders at the gate," where wisdom and justice are dispensed.

In this chapter, let's look at another outsider to the faith in Israel, this time someone who was part of the occupying force maintaining Roman rule in Galilee. We do not know his name, but only his rank as the centurion whose servant Jesus healed.

### Who Was This Man?

First, let's read a brief account of the encounter:

When Jesus had finished saying all this to the people

> who were listening, he entered Capernaum. There a centurion's servant, whom his master valued highly, was sick and about to die. The centurion heard of Jesus and sent some elders of the Jews to him, asking him to come and heal his servant. When they came to Jesus, they pleaded earnestly with him, "This man deserves to have you do this, because he loves our nation and has built our synagogue." So Jesus went with them.
>
> He was not far from the house when the centurion sent friends to say to him: "Lord, don't trouble yourself, for I do not deserve to have you come under my roof. That is why I did not even consider myself worthy to come to you. But say the word, and my servant will be healed. For I myself am a man under authority, with soldiers under me. I tell this one, 'Go,' and he goes; and that one, 'Come,' and he comes. I say to my servant, 'Do this,' and he does it." When Jesus heard this, he was amazed at him, and turning to the crowd following him, he said, "I tell you, I have not found such great faith even in Israel." Then the men who had been sent returned to the house and found the servant well (Luke 7:1-10).

John the Baptist admonished the soldiers in Luke 3:14 to "rob no one by violence or by false accusation and be content with your wages." From that, we can surmise that soldiers often used their position and power to extort money from the powerless. This centurion did the exact opposite, having built a synagogue for the locals, probably one where Jesus had taught. This military man had used his power to empower others, which already qualifies him for the Proverbs 31 moniker.

The Jewish leaders testified to this man's love, which led him to be active in social justice despite the fact that his nation and military had often promoted no such practices. The Jews actually interceded with Jesus on behalf of this man, which was remarkable in and of itself, for the Jews for the most part resented Rome's presence in their land. Then the centurion distinguished himself even further by doing something that caused Jesus to commend him for his great faith.

## Great Faith

The centurion sent word for Jesus not to proceed to his home, for he was not worthy to receive him. Perhaps he knew his home was not kosher, and he did not want to defile Jesus. As a military man, he understood the issue of authority and knew that he, the centurion, did not have to be present for his orders to be obeyed. He could just send his word, and he had faith that Jesus could do the same. What's more, he was asking for healing not for himself or his family, but for his trusted servant, whom he must have loved greatly. In fact, this centurion seemed to have a compassionate, loving heart for many people, Jew and Gentile alike.

This centurion literally took Jesus' breathe away because he had faith—practical, living, common-sense faith. The centurion reasoned in his mind and came to the conclusion that Jesus could heal from a distance and then acted out his belief by preventing Jesus from coming any further than He had. Jesus shook His head in wonder and said something about him he said about no one else.

What have you done lately to build relationships with those who do not have your privilege or wealth? What practical steps have you taken to show your love for those among whom you live or work? When is the last time your faith took Jesus' breath away? What faith conclusions are you coming to and how are you walking them out?

The centurion qualifies on all points that he was a Proverbs 31 man and Jesus gave him a two-thumbs-up endorsement. That is what I want as well, which I think also comes in the words, "Well done, good and faithful servant." Let it be so, Lord Jesus!

# CHAPTER 20

## Alms and Prayers

My goal in this Proverbs 31 series has been to highlight lesser-known men in Scripture who embodied any or all of these four principles:

1. Using leadership power to benefit and not harm those who are weaker.
2. Being concerned for social justice.
3. Honoring women.
4. Serving in leadership capacities as "elders at the gate," where wisdom and justice are dispensed.

I do this so men will read, learn from these examples, and then take their places in the world as their own version of a Proverbs 31 man. In this chapter, let's look at another Roman military officer, this one stationed at Caesarea on the coast, but still under the command of Herod and Caesar. He was there as part of a police force to maintain order and his name was Cornelius.

### Who Was This Man?

We learn what we know of this man in Acts 10:

> At Caesarea there was a man named Cornelius, a centurion in what was known as the Italian Regiment. He and all his family were devout and God-fearing; he gave generously to those in need and prayed to God regularly. One day at about three in the afternoon he had a vision. He distinctly saw an angel of God, who came to him and said, "Cornelius!" Cornelius stared at him in fear. "What is it, Lord?" he asked. The angel answered, "Your prayers and gifts to the poor have come up as a memorial offering before God. Now send men to Joppa to bring back a man named Simon who is called Peter. He is staying with Simon the tanner, whose house is by the sea." When the angel who spoke to him had gone, Cornelius called two of his servants and a devout soldier who was one of his attendants. He told them everything that had happened and sent them to Joppa (Acts 10:1-8).

There is much to consider from this passage. Cornelius was walking in light and truth apart from the Jewish religion and nation. He prayed and gave money to the poor and had gone as far as he could go spiritually without Christ. Therefore, an angel appeared to him to direct him, but could not lead him to the waters of baptism. Peter had to do that. Obviously this man had been seeking the Lord about direction for his life, for the angel said Peter would tell him what to do (see Acts 10:22).

It is of note that Cornelius' good deeds had come before God as a memorial, which speaks to the power of the spiritual practices of prayer and generosity. What's more, this man's faith in God had infected his entire household and workforce, for he sent two servants and a devout soldier to summon Peter, who was 30 miles away in Joppa.

### Managing His Household

Paul later described the qualifications for those who would serve as elders in the church of God. One of those requirements was outlined in 1 Timothy 3:4: "He must manage his own family well and see that his children obey him, and he must do so in a manner worthy of full respect." We do not know if Cornelius had children, but we do know that many of his relatives relocated to Judea and made their home there just so they could be close to him. He rewarded their loyalty and they respected and responded to his leadership when they assembled at his direction:

> The following day he arrived in Caesarea. Cornelius was expecting them and had called together his relatives and close friends. As Peter entered the house, Cornelius met him and fell at his feet in reverence. But Peter made him get up. "Stand up," he said, "I am only a man myself." While talking with him, Peter went inside and found a large gathering of people (Acts 10:24-27).

Cornelius had power but he did not abuse that power because he feared God. He used his power and position to influence those around him and, when it mattered most, to lead them to the truth found only in Christ. The Holy Spirit was so pleased with what He beheld in this man that He moved on the assembly while Peter was still preaching and filled them all with His presence. I would assume that women and children were among the gathering that day for the Gentile Pentecost.

We need Proverbs 31 men today who will manage their households as Cornelius did his. A man's family knows him best of all, and that proximity will either produce a cohesive family culture that includes faith or a divisive culture that alienates members. Where single-parent homes led by women exist, those same men must do what they can to help those women have a male presence in their households—and the single mothers should accept the importance of that presence as well. Where the family cannot provide that presence, then the Church should do what it can.

There are plenty of examples of men in the Bible who

abused their power and strength and would therefore not qualify to be listed in the Proverbs 31 category, but Cornelius is one who does. What can you learn from his life? If nothing else, you should see that God observes your daily good deeds and spiritual disciplines. They ascend to heaven as a memorial and they mean something to Him. I urge you to be a Proverbs 31 man (or woman) whom God can call on not only to impart truth but also to be in a position to share that truth with those closest to you.

# CHAPTER 21

## A Friend Indeed

In the next two chapters, I want to look at a man who may be better known than most in this collection of stories. His name is Jonathan, the beloved friend of King David. Let's learn what made him a candidate to earn the label of a Proverbs 31 man.

### Who Was This Man?

I assume you are aware of the saga that features King Saul, Jonathan, and David. If not, you can read about them in 1 Samuel and 2 Samuel. There we learn that Saul was chosen to be Israel's first king, but because of his disobedience, God rejected him and chose to anoint another man to succeed him who was after God's own heart. The problem was that Saul was still on the throne and did not take kindly to the idea of his successor being around. Even though David was his son-in-law, Saul did not hesitate to pursue David with murderous intent.

It is remarkable that Jonathan, who was Saul's son and heir apparent to the throne, befriended David in the midst of his father's campaign against David. We read in 1 Samuel 18:1-4,

> After David had finished talking with Saul, Jonathan became one in spirit with David, and he loved him as himself. From that day Saul kept David with him and did not let him return home to his family. And Jonathan made a covenant with David because he loved him as himself. Jonathan took off the robe he was wearing and gave it to David, along with his tunic, and even his sword, his bow and his belt.

It was the custom for the older son to become king after his father's death. Jonathan did not see David as a threat, however, but rather as a friend and covenant brother. He symbolically clothed his friend with his prince's garb to identify David as a special, anointed leader. Later, when David was fleeing from Jonathan's father to save his life, Jonathan encouraged David with these words:

> "Don't be afraid," he said. "My father Saul will not lay a hand on you. You will be king over Israel, and I will be second to you. Even my father Saul knows this." The two of them made a covenant before the Lord. Then Jonathan went home, but David remained at Horesh (1 Samuel 23:17-18).

Jonathan clearly and publicly acknowledged God's plan that David's purpose was to be king and Jonathan's role was to serve him as his right-hand man. Jonathan was relinquishing his claim to the throne and expressing his willingness to accept the position and purpose God had for him. I find this truly amazing and it qualifies Jonathan as a special man a Proverbs 31 man.

### More Qualifications

On two occasions prior to these meetings with David, Jonathan had distinguished himself as a wise leader who was better equipped than his father to lead. One instance was when Saul put the army under a curse if anyone ate anything before their battle was over and won. Not knowing this, Jonathan ate some honey, and when he was told of his father's words, he replied,

> "My father has made trouble for the country. See how my eyes brightened when I tasted a little of this honey. How much better it would have been if the men had eaten today some of the plunder they took from their enemies. Would not the slaughter of the Philistines have been even greater?" (1 Samuel 14:29-30).

Jonathan was a better commander and handler of men than his father. Prior to the honey incident, Jonathan had led the people to a great victory by attacking the Philistines even though no one had a weapon but Jonathan:

> Jonathan climbed up, using his hands and feet, with his armor-bearer right behind him. The Philistines fell before Jonathan, and his armor-bearer followed and killed behind him. In that first attack Jonathan and his armor-bearer killed some twenty men in an area of about half an acre (1 Samuel 14:13-14).

I would argue that Jonathan qualifies as a Proverbs 31 man because he used his leadership power and position not to build his own kingdom but to establish David's. What's more, Jonathan opposed his father on more than one occasion, standing up to the powerful on behalf of the weak and standing in the gap for others when his father was a coward. Jonathan was interested in God's justice and not that of his flawed father, so he sided with the Lord and His anointed in the nation of Israel. Jonathan was quite a man and fulfilled the old adage that says, "a friend in need is a friend indeed." In the next chapter, we will see, however, that the vision Jonathan had for his role in David's kingdom never came to pass, and we will learn why.

For now, I want to address men and challenge them to be a Jonathan wherever you are. Stand against tyrants even if they are closely related to you. Encourage others in the will of God for their lives even if it costs you something—or they are in a position you want or hoped to have. Don't crave power or position, but instead actively search for ways to serve others. Take your place as a servant to those over you, not in silly or slavish ways, but by adding your strength to their strength to stand for justice and unity. Imagine what the church and world would be like if men renounced power, resisted envy, and ran in their God-assigned lanes, using their strength and position for the good of others. What a wonderful world that would be.

# CHAPTER 22

## For This Reason, A Man Shall Leave

In Chapter 21, we looked at the relationship between Jonathan and David. Jonathan saw David's future, which included the throne that Saul was occupying, and Jonathan affirmed and endorsed David's claim to that throne according to God's will. We saw Jonathan's remarkable words to David when he was discouraged:

> "Don't be afraid," he said. "My father Saul will not lay a hand on you. You will be king over Israel, and I will be second to you. Even my father Saul knows this." The two of them made a covenant before the Lord. Then Jonathan went home, but David remained at Horesh (1 Samuel 23:17-18).

Even though Jonathan knew his place and boldly proclaimed it, that scenario sadly never came to pass. Let's look at the reason it didn't.

### An Untimely Death

Jonathan never took his place next to David because

he died in battle alongside his father and brothers: "The Philistines pressed hard after Saul and his sons, and they killed his sons Jonathan, Abinadab and Malki-Shua" (1 Samuel 31:2). I have a question at this point. With the knowledge Jonathan had about his future with David, what was he doing with his worthless father, going into a battle they could not win?

Some people have answered that Jonathan was staying loyal to his father, the authority on the throne. Yet we know others had left their place to join David and wander with him as the king in transient exile. Others have told me that the Lord didn't direct Jonathan to go, and indeed the Bible would bear this out. Yet, did God need to tell Jonathan to join himself physically to the man to whom God had spiritually and practically joined him? Still others replied that Jonathan was a prince and belonged in the house of the king. I reject all such answers.

I say Jonathan could not bring himself to stand against his family, even though God had showed him the family head was murderous and actively at war with God's will for the throne. I don't think God needed to send Jonathan an engraved invitation to leave. The door was open, but Jonathan could not bring himself to "leave his father and mother" and join himself to David, "forsaking all others," as we say at weddings. Because Jonathan could not deal with his father or the price he would pay to stand with David, he forfeited his right to fulfill his purpose. He died and David mourned him for the rest of his life. What's more, David never had a second-in-command during his reign because the man who was to serve in that capacity could not break with his family culture.

## The Implications for You

We are examining Jonathan's life to determine if he was a Proverbs 31 man. I concluded in the last chapter that he was, yet Jonathan's impact was limited because of his family. What does this have to do with you? It is important that you, as a Proverbs 31 man (or woman), follow God's will for your life and not let relationships sidetrack you. You cannot allow your supervisor, pastor, friends, children, spouse, or family to hinder you from pursuing and fulfilling your purpose.

I hope you are not facing a situation as difficult as the one presented to Saul, Jonathan, and David. No matter how tough the situation, however, you must steward your purpose and do so on an ongoing basis. You must oversee it and not allow anyone to talk you out of it, or keep you from being the fullest, best expression of who God created you to be.

It's time to take an honest look at your life and purpose. Have you listened to a negative, discouraging report from someone about you and your abilities? Have you put your purpose on the shelf to please or serve someone else? Have you spent time trying to tell God why you aren't the one to do what it is that is in your heart? Has your family become more important than God's purpose for your life?

As you answer these questions, please remember Jonathan who knew his purpose but lost it because he could not admit his father was a scoundrel who did not have anyone's best interests at heart but his own. You will answer to no one but God for the results of what He has assigned you to do. I urge you to determine in your heart that your top priority is to please Him and not family bonds or traditions.

# CHAPTER 23

## The Son of Encouragement

Just a few chapters to go, so let's finish strong and learn our final lessons that can make us all Proverbs 31 people, even though our focus has been men throughout this book. In this chapter, let's look at the life of a man named Joseph. You probably don't know him as Joseph, because his name was changed by the apostles. We know him as Barnabas and the story of how he got that nickname is a great study in the concept of purpose.

### Who Was This Man?

We read in Acts 4:36-37 "Joseph, a Levite from Cyprus, whom the apostles called Barnabas (which means Son of Encouragement), sold a field he owned and brought the money and put it at the apostles' feet." Put yourself in the apostles' place in those early days. They were informed that someone wanted to see them and perhaps their heart sank since they were hoping to finish their day and go home. When they heard it was Joseph, however, they perked up and said, "Oh, you mean Barnabas, the son of encouragement. Every time we see him, he encourages us. Show him in."

At that point, Joseph came in holding two bags of money and placed them at the apostles' feet. He said, "I had this piece of land, but as a Levite I am technically not supposed to own anything, for the Lord is our portion as His servants. I thought I would sell it and give the money to you to do with as you wish. I appreciate the job you're doing, and I love you all."

When he left, the apostles were glad they had let him in. As they expected, he refreshed and encouraged them and was true to the new name he had been given. From that point on, every time we read of Barnabas, he was living up to his name, which embodied his purpose to encourage others.

When the early church leaders would not have anything to do with Saul, Barnabas came forward and encouraged them to accept him (see Acts 9:27). When the work in Antioch among the Gentiles was exploding, the apostles sent Barnabas there:

> When he arrived and saw the evidence of the grace of God, he was glad and *encouraged* them all to remain true to the Lord with all their hearts. He was a good man, full of the Holy Spirit and faith, and a great number of people were brought to the Lord (Acts 11:23-24, emphasis added).

Barnabas wasn't interested in keeping that work in Antioch all to himself, so he "went to Tarsus to look for Saul, and when he found him, he brought him to Antioch" (Acts 11:25-26) Barnabas took that opportunity to encourage Saul and his ministry after he encouraged the new church at Antioch. Barnabas had more than a gift of encouragement, for he was a teacher, apostle, prophet, evangelist, and giver. Yet he always found a way to encourage others, no matter what he was doing.

### True to His Purpose

Eventually, Joseph's commitment to his purpose cost him and his ministry something:

> Some time later Paul said to Barnabas, "Let us go

> back and visit the believers in all the towns where we preached the word of the Lord and see how they are doing." Barnabas wanted to take John, also called Mark, with them, but Paul did not think it wise to take him, because he had deserted them in Pamphylia and had not continued with them in the work. They had such a sharp disagreement that they parted company. Barnabas took Mark and sailed for Cyprus . . . (Acts 15:36-39).

John Mark was Barnabas' cousin and the Son of Encouragement could not bring himself to discourage his cousin by not giving him a second chance. Therefore, Barnabas stood up to Paul, left the team, and took his cousin back to their home area of Cyprus.

Throughout this book, I have considered someone a Proverbs 31 man if they could meet one or more of these criteria:

1. Using leadership power to benefit and not harm those who are weaker.
2. Being concerned for social justice.
3. Honoring women.
4. Serving in leadership capacities as "elders at the gate," where wisdom and justice are dispensed.

I conclude that Barnabas qualifies based on numbers one and four. He was wise and used his power not to harm others but to help and serve them again and again. Perhaps he knew his cousin had left the team because of Paul's domineering ways, or because the team had started out Barnabas and Saul but then became Paul and all the others. The team had also encountered danger along the way and maybe John Mark was afraid. Whatever his reason for leaving, Barnabas wanted to encourage Mark and allow him back on the team because that is who he was at the core of his being: the Son of Encouragement.

Proverbs 31 men and women know their purpose and from that knowledge make a place for themselves that is personally fulfilling while also beneficial to others. We need more people like Barnabas who will devote their lives to uplift and inspire others, not just to feel better when they are down, but to challenge and encourage them to find and fulfill their purpose. If that is what you want to do, then I encourage you (Barnabas would be happy I wrote that) to be true to who you are, even if it seems like it is so basic that anyone could do it. The truth is, they cannot, but you can and when you do, the world will be a better place.

# CHAPTER 24

## On the Move

In this chapter, let's look at Joseph, the earthly father of Jesus. I want to say as we start that Joseph qualifies as a Proverbs 31 man. One of the stipulations to qualify for that category is that the man being considered honored women and used his life and strength to serve others. Joseph obviously did all that, but there is much more we can learn from him even though the Bible says very little about him. The little it does reveal, however, gives us a good idea of why this man was chosen to be Jesus' earthly father.

### Who Was This Man?

Joseph was a carpenter or more probably a general contractor, for there would not have been much wood in Palestine then as today. He lived in Nazareth and could trace his lineage to the tribe of Judah (Matthew 1:16), specifically to the house of David (Matthew 1:20). This is significant, for many Jews lost the trail of their ancestry, so to speak, after the Babylonian captivity. It is also important to note that Joseph was a righteous man, which was a rarity in those days, so much so that Matthew felt compelled to report that aspect of who Joseph was.

Yet how did Joseph's righteousness manifest itself? Through large offerings from his business? Through meticulous obedience to the Law through sacrifice? Through a study of God's Law as a rabbi or scholar? No, it was none of those things. He showed his righteousness by his response when he discovered Mary, his betrothed, was pregnant: "Because Joseph her husband was faithful to the law, and yet did not want to expose her to public disgrace, he had in mind to divorce her quietly" (Matthew 1:19).

Oh, that more men and women would act like Joseph when they perceive a wrong or receive a hurt—but that is not what made Joseph one of the best examples of a Proverbs 31 man in the Bible. What I want to look at is the fact that Joseph was always on the move.

### In Motion

As we study the few verses that mention Joseph, we learn he was always in motion, going somewhere to do God's bidding or at God's direction:

1. When he had his first dream informing him Mary was pregnant by the Spirit, he immediately awoke and went to take her as his wife (Matthew 1:24).
2. When Caesar ordered a census, Joseph left Nazareth and traveled to Bethlehem (Luke 2:4).
3. When Jesus was eight days old, Joseph traveled from Bethlehem to Jerusalem to present Him in the Temple (Luke 2:22). Joseph named the baby Jesus, which is what the angel instructed Mary to name Him. (Please note that Joseph had to submit to God's work in his wife's life.)
4. After the Magi came and alerted Herod, Joseph had a second dream warning him to take Mary and Jesus to Egypt (Matthew 2:13-15).
5. When Herod died, Joseph had a third dream

# CHAPTER 25

## The Reformer

This is the last chapter in our Proverbs 31 Men study. We have looked at 22 men who embodied and exemplified the characteristics of a godly man described in Proverbs 31. I summarized those characteristics in four traits:

1. Using leadership power to benefit and not harm those who are weaker.
2. Being concerned for social justice.
3. Honoring women.
4. Serving in leadership capacities as "elders at the gate," where wisdom and justice are dispensed.

For our final chapter, let's look at one of the last kings of Judah before the Babylonian captivity whose name was Josiah (or Josias). You can read his story in 2 Kings 22-23:30.

**Who Was This Man?**

When we first meet Josiah, he was not yet an adult but rather an eight-year-old child who became king after his father was assassinated. He reigned for 31 years and was considered a good king, even though Judah was too far gone spiritually at that point to be spared God's judgment: "He did what was right in the eyes of the Lord and followed completely the ways of his father David, not turning aside to the right or to the left" (2 Kings 22:2).

As men carried out Josiah's directive to cleanse the Temple from idolatry, they discovered a book, the Law or the Bible of the day, which had been lost as Temple worship had deteriorated into idolatry and chaos. We read,

> Then Shaphan the secretary informed the king, "Hilkiah the priest has given me a book." And Shaphan read from it in the presence of the king. When the king heard the words of the Book of the Law, he tore his robes" (2 Kings 22:10-11).

From that point, Josiah determined not only to cleanse the Temple but also the whole land of its idolatrous practices and was encouraged in his efforts by a woman prophet named Huldah. I don't remember ever hearing her name mentioned in any sermon or teaching on the prophetic, by the way. Huldah delivered the word of the Lord, which was in effect that God would honor Josiah even though it was too late to save Judah. They were too far gone, and God had already initiated His judgment:

> "Tell the king of Judah, who sent you to inquire of the Lord, 'This is what the Lord, the God of Israel, says concerning the words you heard: Because your heart was responsive and you humbled yourself before the Lord when you heard what I have spoken against this place and its people—that they would become a curse and be laid waste—and because you tore your robes and wept in my presence, I also have heard you, declares the Lord'" (2 Kings 22:18-19).

Josiah was a great spiritual reformer but lost his life when he decided to try his hand on the battlefield, being defeated by the Egyptian leader Necho. Necho had warned

Josiah not to attack him—but Josiah did not heed his warning and lost his life.

## Does He Qualify?

Despite his machismo that motivated him to fight a battle not belonging to him, thus forfeiting his life, Josiah certainly qualifies as a Proverbs 31 man. He honored women, or at least one woman in particular, when he accepted the word of the Lord through Huldah as described above. Some men have trouble receiving any direction from a woman, but Josiah does not seem to have had that weakness. Yet his greatest accomplishment was in "using leadership power to benefit and not harm those who are weaker." We read in 2 Kings 23:10: "He desecrated Topheth, which was in the Valley of Ben Hinnom, so no one could use it to sacrifice their son or daughter in the fire to Molek."

It is almost incomprehensible Judah had fallen so far away from the Lord that child sacrifice was taking place, but they had and it was. This is why Josiah was too late to save the nation, but he was not too late to save some of its children. Proverbs 31 men use their power to empower and protect others, especially the weak and powerless, and Josiah acted wisely when he took aggressive action to protect the children in the land.

My reason for writing this book is my observation that women tend to be more active and engaged in modern churches than men. It's not that men don't attend church, but they tend not to get involved beyond that—unless there is some leadership title attached to the work. That is a gross overgeneralization, but it is fair to say that unless men who understand the principles described in Proverbs 31 are actively engaged in missions, teaching youth and children, and leading their homes, unscrupulous men outside the church will continue to wreak havoc on the righteous.

I urge you if you are of the male persuasion not to be a passive worshiper and follower of Christ. Don't use your time or dedicate the best of who you are to sports, entertainment, or trivial hobbies. Give yourself to things that matter, things that serve the best interests of others. The Church will thrive when both women *and* men see their role as essential not just in public worship but in public and private practice. May the words of the song I quoted earlier in this series become a reality in my lifetime and yours:

> *Rise up, oh men of God, have done with lesser things. Give heart and soul and mind and strength, to serve the King of kings.*
>
> *Rise up, oh men of God, His Kingdom tarries long. Bring in the day of brotherhood, and end the night of wrong.*
>
> *Rise up, oh men of God, the Church for you doth wait. Send forth to serve the needs of men, in Christ our strength is great.*
>
> *Lift high the Cross of Christ, tread where His feet have trod. As brothers of the Son of Man, rise up oh men of God.*

# Conclusion

My purpose in writing this book was to stimulate, motivate, and inspire men to rise up and take their place in the Church. It is ironic, however, that I would appeal for men to be more involved through reading a book, when men who are not motivated to serve will probably also not be motivated to read—especially a book that is encouraging them to do more, take more risks, and step out of their comfort zones to perform missions and accept leadership positions.

I am used to writing in faith, however, and often think of a story I heard about the composer Beethoven who was so discouraged with the lack of response to his music by his peers that he stopped writing for them and began composing for a future audience. Of course, we are that future audience and we appreciate Beethoven obviously more than his contemporaries did. I may also be writing for a future time when God's Spirit stirs the waters in men's hearts. When He does, my book will hopefully serve the purpose for which it was written.

I also think of the saying, "You must become the change you seek." I have seen that quote attributed to numerous people, but it is not important to me who said it. It has become important to me to live it and this book has served as a statement of what I believe for my own life. It is vital that I accept my role in the Church and my world, and that means I must write, broadcast, influence, serve, and grow until I have no strength left to do any of it. All I can do is set an example, try to influence in both word and deed, and trust the Lord for the results.

If you share my burden to see more men involved in the work of the Lord, then I urge you to invest a copy of this book into the lives of another man. If you are a sister in the Lord, I recommend you do the same with my book, *The Power of Purpose: Women of Purpose in Scripture.* Together, we can make a difference that will help fill the vacant spaces for service that remain open in God's plan. And of course, we can all pray as Jesus taught us to do:

> Jesus went through all the towns and villages, teaching in their synagogues, proclaiming the good news of the kingdom and healing every disease and sickness. When he saw the crowds, he had compassion on them, because they were harassed and helpless, like sheep without a shepherd. Then he said to his disciples, "The harvest is plentiful but the workers are few. Ask the Lord of the harvest, therefore, to send out workers into his harvest field" (Matthew 9:35-38).

Thank you for reading and may God raise up workers for the harvest of purpose that is and is yet to come.

# About the Author

John Stanko was born in Pittsburgh, Pennsylvania. After graduating from St. Basil's Prep School in Stamford, Connecticut, he attended Duquesne University where he received his bachelor's and master's degrees in eco-nomics in 1972 and 1974 respectively.

Since then, John has served as an administrator, teacher, consultant, author, and pastor in his profession-al career. He holds a second master's degree in pastoral ministries, and earned his doctorate in pastoral ministries from Liberty Theological Seminary in Houston, Texas in 1995. He recently completed a second doctor of ministry degree at Reformed Presbyterian Theological Seminary in Pittsburgh.

John has taught extensively on the topics of time management, life purpose and organization, and has conducted leadership and purpose training sessions throughout the United States and in 32 countries. He is also certified to administer the DISC and other relat-ed personality assessments as well as the Natural Church Development profile for churches. In 2006, he earned the privilege to facilitate for The Pacific Institute of Seattle, a leadership and personal development program, and for The Leadership Circle, a provider of cultural and executive 360-degree profiles. He has authored fifteen books and written for many publications around the world.

John founded a personal and leadership devel-op-ment company, called PurposeQuest, in 2001 and today travels the world to speak, consult and inspire lead-ers and people everywhere. From 2001-2008, he spent six months a year in Africa and still enjoys visiting and working on that continent, while teaching for Geneva College's Masters of Organizational Leadership and the Center for Urban Biblical Ministry in his hometown of Pittsburgh, Pennsylvania. John has been married for 38 years to Kathryn Scimone Stanko, and they have two adult children. In 2009, John was appointed the ad-min-istra-tive pastor for discipleship at Allegheny Center Alliance Church on the North Side of Pittsburgh where he served for five years. Most recently, John founded Urban Press, a publishing service designed to tell stories of the city, from the city and to the city.

# Keep in Touch with John Stanko

www.purposequest.com
www.johnstanko.us
www.stankobiblestudy.com
www.stankomondaymemo.com
or via email at johnstanko@gmail.com

John also does extensive relief and community develop-ment work in Kenya. You can see some of his projects at www.purposequest.com/contributions

PurposeQuest International
PO Box 8882
Pittsburgh, PA 15221-0882

# Additional Titles by John Stanko

A Daily Dose of Proverbs
A Daily Taste of Proverbs
A String of Pearls
Changing the Way We Do Church
I Wrote This Book on Purpose
Life Is A Gold Mine: Can You Dig It?
Strictly Business
The Faith Files, Volume 1
The Faith Files, Volume 2
The Faith Files, Volume 3
The Leadership Walk
The Price of Leadership
Unlocking the Power of Your Creativity
Unlocking the Power of Your Productivity Unlocking the Power of Your Purpose
Unlocking the Power of You
What Would Jesus Ask You Today?
Your Life Matters

Made in the USA
Monee, IL
04 November 2026

67379931R00066